THE SOCIAL FUTURE

THE
SOCIAL FUTURE

By
Rudolf Steiner

ANTHROPOSOPHIC PRESS, INC.
Spring Valley, New York

The six lectures presented here were given in
Zurich, October 24–30, 1919, under the title,
Soziale Zukunft. Translated by Henry B. Monges
from German shorthand reports unrevised by
the lecturer.

First edition, 1935
Second edition, revised, 1945
Third edition, revised, 1972

CONTENTS

EDITORS' NOTE

Due to the evergrowing demand for constructive approaches to the social problems of our time, the Anthroposophic Press herewith offers a new edition of a translation of six lectures given by Rudolf Steiner the year after the end of World War I. These lectures supplement his book, *Die Kernpunkte der sozialen Frage*, first published in 1919 and available in English translation under the titles, *The Threefold Commonwealth* and *The Threefold Social Order* (Anthroposophic Press, 1972).

Contemporary history shows that when society is dominated by a totalitarian political state, individual freedom is lost. A society built on economic interest and technology alone breeds social unrest and leads to a starvation of the cultural life from which man should receive inspiration and enlightenment. These lectures on "The Social Future" show that The Threefold Social Order can bring about a healthy social organism that will overcome the polarizing tendencies of modern life and make the economy the servant of society rather than its master. We therefore believe that these lectures will be found to be as timely today as they were fifty years ago when they were given.

THE SOCIAL FUTURE

I

THE SOCIAL QUESTION
AS A CULTURAL QUESTION, A QUESTION OF EQUITY AND A QUESTION OF ECONOMICS.

The social question should not be regarded as a mere party matter nor as a problem resulting from the personal demands of a few individuals. It has arisen in the course of social evolution and belongs to the facts of history. One of these facts is the proletarian socialist movement that has been growing steadily for more than half a century.

According to our own views of life or our circumstances, we may regard the conceptions coming to light in this socialist proletarian movement either critically or approvingly. But whatever our attitude towards it is, we can only accept it as an historic fact that must be dealt with as such. Whoever reflects on the terrible years of the so-called World War,* even though he may feel compelled to see causes and motives of different kinds for these horrors, must acknowledge that it is the social demands, the social contrasts that

---

* (World War I.)

3

have to a great extent caused them. Especially now that we are at the end, at least for the present, of those terrible events, it must be clearly evident to everyone that over a great part of the civilized world the social question has sprung to life as a result of the World War. If the social question has sprung to life as a result of the World War, there is little doubt that it was already concealed within it.

Now it will be impossible for anyone to judge this question rightly who regards it from his own narrow, often personal standpoint as is so frequently done today. No one who cannot widen his horizon to take in the events of human life as a whole is able to take an impartial view of the social question, and it is just that widening of our horizon that is aimed at in my book, *The Threefold Commonwealth* (*Die Kernpunkte der Sozialen Frage*).

We must remember, too, that most people who speak on the social question today quite naturally regard it in the first place as a question of economics; it is even looked upon purely as a question of food, or, at best, as facts plainly demonstrate, as one of labor—a question of food and labor. If we are to regard this question merely in the light of a food and labor question, we must remember that the human being is supplied with bread because it is produced for him by the community at large, and that bread can only be produced by labor. But the manner in which that labor should and must be carried on depends in every respect upon the manner in which human society or any separate part of it, for instance, a country, is organized. To anyone who has acquired a wider outlook on life it will be clear that there can be no rise or fall in the price of a piece of bread without the occurrence of great, of immense changes in the whole structure of the social organism. To anyone who observes attentively the manner in which the individual worker plays

4

his part in the social organism, it becomes evident that when a man works but a quarter of an hour more or less, this fact is expressed in the way in which the society of any economic region procures bread and money for the individual. You see from this that, even if we regard the social question merely as one of bread and labor, we at once enlarge our horizon, and it is of this wider horizon in its most varied aspects that I should like to speak to you in these six lectures. Today, before going further, I would like to make a few introductory remarks.

When we survey the latest history of the evolution of the human race, we soon find confirmation of what has been so impressively stated by discriminating observers of social life; of course, this applies only to discriminating observers. There is a publication of the year 1910 that contains, it may be said, the best that has been written on this subject and that is the outcome of a real insight into social conditions. It is the work of Hartley Withers, *Money and Credit*. The author acknowledges pretty frankly that everyone who professes to deal with the social question at all at the present day should keep in mind that the manner in which credit, property, and money conditions figure in the social organism is so complicated as to have a bewildering effect. If we try logically to analyze the functions of credit, money, labor, etc., Withers tells us, it is an absolute impossibility to collect the material necessary to follow with understanding the things that arise within the social organism. What has been here stated with so much insight is confirmed by the whole volume of historical thought in modern times on the social problem, and especially on the social and economic co-operation of human beings.

What, then, is really the conclusion at which we have arrived? Since the time when the economic life of a country ceased to have institutions of an instinctively patriarchal character, ever since the economic life began to assume a more complicated form under the influence of modern technical science and modern capitalism, the necessity has been felt to consider the economic side of life scientifically, and to form such ideas with regard to it as are usually applied in scientific research or study. We have seen how in modern times views have arisen regarding national, or political, economy, as it is called, to which the words 'mercantilistic' or 'physiocratic' have been applied, views such as those of Adam Smith, etc., down to Marx, Engels, Blanc, Fourier, Saint-Simon, and on to the present day. What has come to light in the course of this national economic thought? Let us look at the school of thought known as the mercantilistic, or at the physiocratic school of national economy, and let us examine what Ricardo, the teacher of Karl Marx, has contributed to the study of national economy. We may also examine what many other economists have said and we shall always find that these men turn their attention to one or another particular line of thought in the phenomena of economics. From this one-sided standpoint they endeavor to arrive at certain laws according to which the economic life of a nation can be molded. The result has always shown that laws that have thus been discovered according to the methods of scientific thought can be adapted to some facts of national economy, but that other facts are found to be too far-reaching for comprehension within these laws. It has always been demonstrated that the views of those who, in the seventeenth, eighteenth, and the beginning of the nineteenth centuries, claimed to have discovered laws, according to which the economic life of a nation can be constituted, were one-sided. Then something remarkable came to pass.

It may be said that national, or political, economy has grown to the status of a science. It has taken its place among the sciences in our universities, and the whole armory of scientific thought has been brought to bear on the investigation of the economic aspect of social life. With what result? What is the answer of Roscher, of Wagner or others to this question? They have arrived at a consideration of economic laws in which they do not dare to formulate maxims or give expression to impulses capable of actually grappling with and forming the economic life. We might say that the role that national economy has taken is that of a contemplative spectator; it has retreated more or less before the activity of social life. It has not discovered laws capable of molding human life within the social organism.

The same thing is seen in another way. We have seen that men have arisen, large-hearted, benevolent, humanitarian, with fraternal feelings towards their fellow men. We need only mention Fourier and Saint-Simon. There are others like them. Model forms of society have been thought out by these distinguished thinkers, the realization of which, they believe, would bring about desirable social conditions in human life.

Now we know how those of the present day think concerning such social ideas who feel the social question to be one of vital importance. If we ask those who may be said to hold really modern socialistic views for their opinion of the social ideals of a Fourier, or a Louis Blanc, or a Saint-Simon, they would say, "These are utopias, pictures of social life through which an appeal to the governing classes is made; if they would act in accordance with these pictures, many evils of social misery would disappear. But all such imaginary utopias are wanting in the force needed to inspire the human will, they can never be anything but utopias. However beautiful the theories put forward may be, human instincts—for instance, those of the wealthy classes—will never alter so as to put those theories into

7

practice. Other forces are needed to bring that about." In short, an absolute unbelief has arisen in the social ideals born of feeling, sentiment and modern learning that have been presented to humanity.

This again hangs together with the general course of events in the cultured life of humanity as seen in the development of modern history. It has often been expressly stated that what we now recognize as the social question is connected in all essentials with the modern capitalistic organization of economic life, and this, again, in its present special form, is the outcome of the preponderance of modern technical science. But there are many points to be considered in this connection and we shall never be able to deal with these unless we take into account that, with the capitalist régime, and with the modern application of technical science, an entirely new attitude of mind has arisen among modern civilized humanity. This new conception of the world has produced great, epoch-making results, especially in the fields of technical and natural science. There is another side to it, however, of which something must be said.

Those of you who are acquainted with my books will not have failed to observe that I am ready to do full justice to, and in no wise deny or criticize unfavorably, the discoveries of modern times through scientific methods of research. I fully recognize what has been done for the progress of humanity by the Copernican world conception, by the science of Galileo, the widening of the horizon of mankind by Giordano Bruno, and much besides. But side by side with modern technical science, with modern capitalism, a gradual change has come about in the old world conception. The new conception of the world has taken on a decidedly intellectual, above all a scientific, character. It is true that some people find it hard to look facts straight in the face, but we need only recall the fact that the scientific world conception, which we now regard with pride, has gradually developed, as we can show, out of old religious, artistic, aesthetic, moral conceptions of the world. These views possessed a certain impelling force applicable to life. One truth, especially, was peculiar to them all. They led man to the consciousness of the spirituality of his own nature. However we may regard those old views, we must agree that they spoke to man of the spirit, so that he felt within himself the living spiritual being as a part of the cosmic spiritual being pulsating through the world, weaving the web of the universe. In the place of this old conception, with its impelling social force giving an impulse to life, another appeared, new and more scientific in its orientation. This new conception was concerned with more or less abstract laws of nature, and facts gained outside man himself by the senses—abstract ideas and facts. Without detracting in the smallest degree from the value of natural science, we may ask what it bestows on humanity, especially what it bestows on man, to help him solve the riddle of his own existence? Natural science tells us much about the interdependence of the phenomena of nature; it reveals much regarding the physical constitution of the human being, but when it attempts to tell us anything about man's innermost being, science overreaches itself. It can give no answer to this question, and it shows ignorance of itself when it even attempts to answer it.

I do not by any means wish to assert that the common consciousness of humanity already has its source in the teachings of modern science. But it is profoundly true that the scientific mode of thought itself proceeds from a certain definite attitude of the modern human soul. One who can penetrate below the surface of life knows that, since the middle of the fifteenth century, something in the attitude of the human soul has changed, when we compare it with former times, and is still changing more and more. He also knows that the conception of the world that we find typically expressed in scientific thought has been diffused increasingly over the whole human race, first over the cities, then all over the land. It is, therefore, no mere achievement of theoretic natural science of which we are speaking, but an inner attitude of the soul, which has gradually taken possession of humanity as a whole since the dawn of modern times. It is a significant coincidence that this scientific world conception made its appearance at the same time as capitalism and modern technical culture. Men were called away from their old handiwork and placed at machines, crowded together in a factory. The machines at which they stand, the factories in which they are crowded together with their fellows, these, governed only by mechanical laws, have nothing to give a man that has any direct relationship to himself as a man. Out of his old handicraft something flowed to him that gave answer to his query regarding human worth and human dignity. The dead machine gives no answer. Modern industrialism is like a mechanical network spun about the man, in the midst of which he stands; it has nothing to give him that he can joyfully share, as did the work at his old handicraft.

In this way an abyss opened between the industrial working-class and the employers of labor, between the capitalist and the workingman of modern times at his machine in the factory. The worker surrounded by machinery could no longer rise to the old faith, the old world conception with its impulse for life. He had broken away from it because he could not reconcile it with the actualities of life. He held to that, and to that only, which had become a part of modern thought, namely, the scientific conception of the world.

What was the effect of this scientific conception of the world on industrial workingmen? It made them feel ever more strongly that what could be presented to them as a true world conception was mere thought, possessing only the reality of thought. Anyone who has lived among modern workingmen and knows the direction taken by social feelings in later times also knows the meaning of a word that occurs repeatedly in proletarian socialist circles—the word 'ideology.'

Under the influences I have just described, intellectual life has come to be regarded by the modern working classes as ideology. They look upon the natural-scientific view of the world as offering food for thoughts only. The old conception had not only thoughts to give; it gave them something that showed them that their own inmost being was one with the whole spiritual world; it confronted them—spirit with spirit. The modern conception had only thoughts to give and above all, it contained no answer to the question regarding man's real nature. It was felt to be ideology. In this way a division arose between the proletariat and the upper classes who had kept the ancient tradition of the time-honored world conceptions of the aesthetic, artistic, religious, moral beliefs of former times. All this the upper classes retained for the satisfaction of their whole nature; while with their heads they accepted the scientific explanation of the world.

The masses of the people, however, had no inclination for the old tradition nor sympathy with it. For them the only reasonable conception of the world was the scientific, and this they accepted as ideology; it was to them a mere thought structure. To them the economic life was the only reality—production, distribution of products, consumption, the manner of acquiring or bequeathing property, etc. Everything else in human life—equity, ethics, science, art, religion—are all as vapor rising in the form of ideology out of the only reality: the economic life. Thus among the masses, intellectual and spiritual life came to be looked upon as ideology. This was the case especially because the leading classes, while they watched the development of the modern economic life and familiarized themselves with it, did not understand how to bring intellectual and spiritual life into the growing complexity of the economic system. They kept to the old tradition of the intellectual and spiritual life of former days. The masses of the people adopted the new cultural life, but it gave them no comfort or nourishment for heart and soul.

A world conception such as this, felt as an ideology that gives rise to the thought that justice, morality, religion, art, science, are a mere superstructure, a phantom hovering over the only reality, over the conditions of production, the economic order of things, may form a subject for thought, but it gives no support in life. However splendid a world conception such as this may be in the contemplation of nature, it leaves the human soul empty and cold. The fruits of the scientific conception of the world are showing themselves in the events of social life in our time.

These social facts cannot be understood if we only take into account the content of human consciousness. People may think consciously, "Why speak to us of the social question as being of a spiritual nature? The truth is that commodities are unevenly distributed. We want equal distribution." People think like this with the brain, but in the unconscious depths of the soul something quite different is stirring. In those depths is stirring what develops unconsciously, because from the consciousness nothing can flow that could fill the soul with a real spiritual content; from that source can come only what leaves it dead, only what is felt to be ideology. The emptiness of modern intellectual life is the first aspect of the social question that we have to recognize; the social question is in its first aspect a spiritual question.

Since this is true, and since an intellectual life has developed that, in the science of economics as taught in the universities, for instance, has reached a merely contemplative stage, and of itself does not evolve principles of social will; since it is true that the greatest philanthropists, such as Saint-Simon, Louis Blanc, Fourier, have conceived social ideas in which no one believes; since everything without exception that arises out of the mind is regarded as utopian, that is, as mere ideology; since it is a historical fact that a life of thought prevails, that gives the impression of a mere superstructure on top of the economic actuality, which does not really penetrate to the facts and is therefore felt to be ideology—then the social question must in its first aspect be treated as a spiritual-cultural question. One question, above all, stands out before us today in letters of flame. How must the human mind be changed, in order that it may learn to master the social question?

We have seen that science has applied its best methods to the study of political economy, and that the result is mere observation without power to reach the social will. On the soil of modern intellectual life a type of mind has arisen, powerless to develop national economy as a groundwork for practical social will. How must the mind be constituted from which a kind of national economy can proceed, capable of forming the groundwork of a truly social will?

We have seen that the great majority of people, when they hear of the social ideals of well-meaning philanthropists, exclaim, "Utopia!" They cannot believe that the human intelligence is strong enough to master social facts. How must the cultural life of a nation be constituted in order that people may learn again to believe that the mind can grasp ideas capable of creating social institutions that will remove certain evils of social life? We have seen that the scientific view of the world is regarded in wide circles as ideology, but ideology alone empties the soul, and generates in its subconscious

13

depths all that we now observe in the bewildering chaotic facts of the social problem. What new form can we give to cultural life, so that it may cease to appear as ideology, so that it may fill the human soul with strength enabling men to work side by side with their fellow men in a really social manner?

We thus see why the social question must be called a cultural question. We see that the modern intellect has not been able to inspire faith in itself, that it has not been able to fill the soul with a satisfying content, but that, on the contrary, as ideology it has desolated the souls of men. In this introduction, treating the subject historically, I should like to show how out of the circumstances of modern life, the social question must be felt in its three aspects as cultural, legal-political, and economic.

Take, for example, what was said not long ago and has often been repeated by a person actively concerned in political life, in the statesmanship of our day, himself a product of the intellectual life of the present day.

With a deep feeling for the social conditions of America in their development since the War of Secession in the sixties of last century, Woodrow Wilson perceived the relationship between the political and legal conditions and those of the economic life. With a considerable amount of unbiased judgment he watched how the great accumulations of capital have grown in consequence of the complication of modern economic life. He saw the formation of trusts and of the great financial companies. He saw how, even in a democratic state, the principle of democracy has tended more and more to disappear before the secret operations of those companies whose interest was served by secrecy, those companies that with their massed capital acquired great power and obtained influence over enormous numbers of people. He always used his eloquence on the side of freedom in face of the growth of power arising out of economic conditions. He knew from a sentiment of true humanity —this must be said—how every single human being has an influence on the facts of social life, how the social life of the community depends upon the manner in which each individual matures for the duties of social life. He showed how important it is for the health of the social body that in the breast of every human being a freedom-loving heart should beat. He pointed out over and over again that political life must become democratic, that power and the means of power must be taken away from the various trusts, that the individual capacities and powers of every human being who possesses such must have free access to the economic, social and political life as a whole. He emphatically declared that his own government, which he evidently regarded as the most advanced, was suffering from the prevailing conditions. Why was this? Because the economic conditions were there—great accumulations of capital, development of economic power, surpassing everything in this domain that had ever existed, even a short time ago. Perfectly new forms of human social life had been brought about by economic changes. An altogether new form of economic life had suddenly been brought into being.

These views are not the outcome of any leaning towards a theory of my own; they are the words of this statesman, one may say of this 'world statesman.' He has declared that the fundamental evil of modern development lies in the fact that, notwithstanding the progress in economic matters, the latter have been controlled by the secret machinations of certain persons, and the idea of justice, of the political life of the community, has not kept pace with economic progress, but has lingered behind at an earlier stage. Woodrow Wilson has clearly stated, "We carry on business under new conditions.

15

We think and legislate for the economic life of the nation from a point of view long out of date, an antiquated standpoint. Nothing new has been developed in our political life, in our laws. These have stood still. We live in an entirely new economic order, while retaining the out-of-date legal and political ideas." These are the words, or nearly so, spoken by Woodrow Wilson himself. In earnest words he demands that the individual shall work for the benefit of the community, not for his own. He points out that, as long as the incongruity between the political and the economic life continues to exist, the requirements of human evolution at the present epoch in history cannot be satisfied, and he subjects the life of society around him to a severe criticism.

I have taken great pains to examine Woodrow Wilson's criticism of modern social conditions, especially those he has in view, the American, and to compare it with other criticisms. (I am going to say something paradoxical, but present conditions often urgently demand a paradox in order to do justice to the realities of our day.) I have tried both as to the outer form and the inner impulses to compare Woodrow Wilson's criticism of society, in the first place as criticism, with that exercised by advanced thinkers and those holding radical, social democratic opinions. Indeed, one may even extend this comparison to the opinions of the most extreme radicals of the Socialist Party in thought and action. If we go no further than the opinions of such men, it may be said that Woodrow Wilson's criticism of the present social order agrees almost word for word with the sentiments expressed even by Lenin and Trotsky, the gravediggers of modern civilization, of whom it may be said that, if their rule continues too long, even in a few places, it will signify the death of modern civilization and must of necessity lead to the destruction of all the attainments of modern civilization. In spite of this we must give expression to the paradox. Woodrow Wilson, who certainly imagined a different reconstruction of social conditions from that of these destroyers of society, directs almost literally the same criticism against the present order as these others, and he comes to the same conclusion that legal and political conceptions in their present form are obsolete, and are no longer fitted to deal with the economic system. Strange to say, when we try to find something positive and to test what Woodrow Wilson has produced in order to construct a new social organism, we find hardly any answer, only a few measures here and there that have even been proposed elsewhere by someone much less scathing in his criticism. He gives no answer to the question relative to the changes necessary in legal matters, in political conceptions and impulses, in order that these may control the demands of modern economic life and render it possible for them to intervene in its activities.

Here we find that out of modern life itself emerges the second aspect of the social question, that of law and equity. A foundation must first be sought for the necessary legal and political conditions for the state that must exist in order to be able to grapple with and dominate modern economic organizations. We ask how a state of rights, political impulses, can be attained that can meet the great demands of the problem. This is the second aspect of the social question.

If we contemplate life itself, we shall find that the social life of man is threefold. Three aspects are clearly distinguished in him when we consider him as a member of human society. If he is to contribute his share, as he certainly must, to the well-being of the social order in modern society, if he is to add to the welfare of the community by co-operation, in the production of values, of commodities, he must first of all possess individual capacity, individual

17

talent, ability. In the second place, he must be able to live at peace with his fellow men and to work harmoniously with them. Thirdly, he must be able to find his proper place, from which he can further the interests of the community by his work, by his activity, by his achievements.

With respect to the first of these the individual is dependent on human society for the development of his capacities and talents, for the training of his intellect, so that the educated intelligence in him may become at the same time his guide in his physical work.

For the second, the individual is dependent on the existence of a social edifice in which he can live in peace and harmony with his fellow men. The first has to do with the cultural side of life. In the following lectures we shall see the dependence of the intellectual life on the first aspect. The second leads us into the domain of equity, and this can only develop in accordance with its own nature, if a social structure has been established that enables people to work together peacefully and labor for one another. The economic aspect, this modern economic organization is compared, as I have described it, by Woodrow Wilson to a man who has outgrown his clothes, so that his limbs protrude on all sides. These outgrown garments represent to Woodrow Wilson the old legal and political conceptions which the economic body has long since outgrown. The growth of the economic organization beyond the old cultural and political organizations was always strongly felt by socialist thinkers, and we need only look at one thing in order to find the forces at work there.

As we know (we shall go into all these matters more minutely afterwards), the modern proletariat is completely under the influence of Marxism, as it is called. Marxism, or the Marxist doctrine of the conversion of the private ownership of means of production into public ownership, has been much modified by followers and opponents of Karl Marx, but Marxism has, nevertheless, a strong influence on the minds, the views of life, of great masses of people of the present day, and it shows itself distinctly in the chaotic social events of our time. If we take up the undoubtedly remarkable and interesting little book by Friedrich Engels, the friend and collaborator of Karl Marx, *Socialism in Its Evolution from Utopia to Science*, and acquaint ourselves with the whole train of thought in this book, we shall see how a socialist thinker regards economics in its relationship to the political and cultural life of modern times. We must fully understand one sentence, for instance, that occurs in a summary in Engels's little book: In future there must be no more governments over men, over individuals, but only leadership by the branches of economic life and control of production.

These are weighty words. They mean that the holders of such views desire that something in the economic life should cease, something that, following the modern evolutionary impulses, has become a part of the economic life. The economic aspect of life has to a great extent overspread everything, because it has outgrown both political and cultural life, and it has acted like a suggestion on the thoughts, feelings, and passions of men. Thus, it becomes ever more evident that the manner in which the business of a nation is carried on determines, in reality, the cultural and political life of the people. It becomes ever more evident that the commercial and industrial magnates, by their position alone, have acquired the monopoly of culture. The economically weak remain the uneducated. A certain connection has become apparent between the economic and the cultural, and between the cultural and the political organizations. The cultural life has gradually become one that does not evolve out of its own inner needs and does not follow its own impulses, but, especially when it is under public administration, as in

19

schools and educational institutions, it receives the form most useful to the political authority. The human being can no longer be judged according to his capacities; he can no longer be developed as his inborn talents demand. Rather is it asked, "What does the State want? What talents are needed for business? How many men are wanted with a particular training?" The teaching, the schools, the examinations are all directed to this end. The cultural life cannot follow its own laws of development; it is adapted to the political and the economic life.

The immediate effect of this tendency, which we have seen especially of late, has been to make the economic system dependent on the political system. Men like Marx and Engels saw this union of economics, politics, and culture; they saw that the new economic life was no longer compatible with the old political form, nor with the old form of culture. They came to the conclusion that the life of rights, the old life of rights, and the cultural life must be excluded from the economic life, but they were led into a singular error of judgment, of which we shall have much to say in these lectures. They regarded the economic life, which they could see with their own eyes, as the sole reality. The cultural life and the life of equity they saw as ideology, and they believed that the economic life could bring forth out of itself the new political, and the new cultural conditions. So the belief arose—the most fatal of errors—that the economic system must be carried on in a definitely ordered manner. If this were done, they thought, then out of that economic system the cultural life, laws, state-life and politics must come of themselves.

How was it possible for this error of judgment to arise? Only because the real structure of human economy, actual labor in the economic system, was concealed behind what is usually called finance. The financial system made its appearance in Europe as an accompaniment of certain events. If we look more deeply into history we shall see that about the time when the Reformation and the Renaissance brought a new spirit into European civilization, treasures of gold and silver were opened up in America that caused an influx of gold and silver, especially from Central and South America, into Europe. What was formerly an exchange of natural products was gradually replaced by the financial system. The natural system of economics could be directed to what the soil yielded, that is to say, to actuality. Under this system the capacity of the individual with his productive powers could be taken into account; that is, his value as a worker and that of the actual substance of the commodity could be seen in proper relationship. We shall see in these lectures how, with the circulation of money, the importance attached to the essential elements in economics gradually disappeared; with the substitution of finance for the system of natural economy, a veil has, as it were, been drawn over the whole economic life; its actual requirements could no longer be perceived. With what does the economic system provide us? With commodities for our consumption. We need not pause today to distinguish between mental and physical commodities, for the former may also be included in the economic system and used for human consumption. The economic system, then, provides commodities and these commodities are values because the individual needs them, because he desires them. The individual must attach a certain value to a commodity, and in this way the latter acquires an objective value within the social body, and this value is closely connected with the subjective valuation resulting from the individual's private judgment. But how is the value of commodities expressed that may be said to represent the importance of these commodities in the social and economic life? It is expressed by the price. We shall have more to say later about value and price; today I will only say that in economic intercourse, indeed, in social intercourse generally, insofar as the buying and selling of products is concerned, the value of the products for the consumer is expressed by the price. It is a great error to confound the value of commodities with the money price, and people will find out by degrees, not by theoretical deliberations, but in practice, that the value of commodities produced by the economic body and what is the result of human, subjective judgment, or of certain social and political conditions, is different from all that is expressed in the price and in the conditions created by money. But the value of commodities has been concealed in recent times by the conditions governing prices.

This lies at the basis of modern social conditions as the third aspect of the social question. People will learn to recognize the social question as an economic question, when they again begin to give due weight to what fixes the actual value of commodities, as compared with all that finds expression in the mere prices. Price standards cannot be maintained, especially in moments of crisis, except when the state, the domain of law, guarantees the value of money, that is, the value of a single commodity. Without entering into any theoretical consideration regarding the result of misunderstanding the difference between price and value, we can cite something that has actually taken place of late. We read in the literature of political economy that long ago in Central Europe and until the end of the Middle Ages the old system of natural economy was in use. This was built up on the mere exchange of commodities, and its place was taken by the financial system, in which current coin represents commodities and in which only the commodity value is actually exchanged for money. But there is something new making its appearance in social life that seems likely to take the place of the financial system. This new element is everywhere at work, but it passes unnoticed as yet. Anyone who can see through the mere figures in his cashbook and ledger, and can read the language of these figures, will find that they do not merely represent the value of commodities, but that the figures often express what we may call the conditions of credit in the newest sense of the word. What a man can do because someone believes him to be capable of it, what can awaken confidence in the man's capacity, this, strange as it may seem, begins to appear ever more frequently in our dull, dry, business life. Look into business books and you will find that as against the mere money values, mutual confidence, belief in human capacity is beginning to be evident. In modern business books, when we know how to read them, a great change is expressed, a social metamorphosis. When it is said that the old natural economy has given place to the financial system, it must now be added that, in the third place, finance is giving way to credit.

With this change the place of an old institution has again been taken by something new. Thereby a new element appears in social life, the value of the human being. The economic body itself, as far as the production of values is concerned, is on the verge of a transformation. It is faced by a problem. This is the third aspect of the social question.

In these lectures we shall have to learn to look at the social question as a cultural question, as one of law, of the state or politics, and as an economic question.

The spirit must give the answer to the question of how men can be made strong and capable, so that a social structure may arise without the present evils, which are unjustifiable.

The second question is: Under the advanced conditions of the present economic life, what is the political system or system of equity that can lead men to live in peace again?

The third is: What social structure will enable each individual to find the place from which he can work for the human community and its welfare, as well as his nature, his talents and capacities permit? We shall be led to the answer by the question: What credit can be attached to the personal value of a human being? Here we see the transformation of the economic system out of new conditions.

A cultural, a political, and an economic problem are all contained in the social question, and we shall see that the smallest detail of that question can only appear in its true light when we look at it as a whole, fundamentally, in these three aspects, cultural, legal-political, and economic.

II

THE ORGANIZATION OF A PRACTICAL ECONOMIC LIFE ON THE ASSOCIATIVE BASIS. TRANSFORMATION OF THE MARKET AND FIXING OF PRICES. MONEY AND TAXATION. CREDIT.

The idea of the three-membered social organism set forth in my book, *The Threefold Commonwealth,* has grown out of perceptions that have ripened in view of the facts of modern social evolution, such as I attempted to describe yesterday. This idea of the threefold ordering of the social body aims at a practical solution of the problems of life and includes nothing utopian. Hence, before writing my book, I presupposed that it would be received with a common instinct for actual facts, and that it would not be judged out of preconceived theories, preconceived party opinions. If what I said yesterday be correct—and it is correct, undoubtedly—namely, that the social facts in the conditions of human life have grown so complicated that it is extremely difficult to survey them, a new method of dealing with the matters under discussion today will be necessary in order to enkindle the general social purpose. In view of this complexity of facts, it is only too comprehensible that there should be, for the time being, no understanding of the economic phenomena, except of such as have come within the experience of individual people. Everything of this nature is dependent upon the whole of economic life, however, and at the present time not only on the economic life of one country, but on that of the entire world. The individual human being will have, quite naturally and comprehensively, to judge the needs of world economy from the experience of his own immediate circle. He will, of course, go astray. Anyone who knows the demands of thought that are in line with strict reality knows also how important it is to approach the phenomena of the world with a certain amount of instinct for the truth, in order to gain fundamental facts of knowledge. Such facts play the same part in life as fundamental truths in the knowledge gained at school.

Were we to try to acquaint ourselves with the whole of economic life in all its details and from it to draw our conclusions concerning the social purpose, we should never come to an end. In fact, we should just as unlikely come to an end as we would were we compelled to review all the details, let us say, of the application of the Pythagorean theorem in the technical field in order to recognize the truth of that theorem. We accept the truths of the Pythagorean theorem through certain inner thought connections with it, and then we know that wherever it can be applied it must hold good. It is also possible to wrestle with the facts of social knowledge, until certain fundamental facts reveal themselves as truths to our consciousness by their inner nature. Our own sense of truth will then enable us to apply these facts everywhere as the occasion demands. In this way I should like my book, *The Threefold Commonwealth*, to be understood out of its own inner nature, out of the inner nature of the social conditions described. Emphatically, the whole idea of the three-membered social organism should be so understood. But I will particularly endeavor in these lectures to show that certain phenomena of social life give force to the conclusions arising from the idea of the threefold membering of the social organism. This idea is a result of the necessities of the present day and of the near future of humanity. I will also show how these confirmations may be arrived at.

First, it will be necessary to recall to you, as an introduction to my subject for today, the fundamental idea of the threefold membering of the social order. We have seen that our social life has three principal roots or members, from which spring its demands—in other words, that it is a question of culture, of state, law, politics, and of economics. Anyone who studies modern evolution will find that these three elements of life, cultural, political, and economic, have intermingled gradually, until they now form a chaotic whole, and out of the amalgamation of these three elements the present evils of society have arisen.

If we thoroughly understand this—and these lectures are intended to help us do so—we shall find that the direction evolution must take in the future will be the ordering of public life and of the social organism so that there will be an independent cultural life, especially as regards general culture, education and teaching, an independent political, legal body, and a completely independent economic body. At present, a single administrative body embraces these three elements of life in our states, and when a three-membering is mentioned it is always misunderstood. It is taken to mean that an independent administration is demanded for the cultural life, another for the political life, and a third for the economic body—three parliaments instead of one. This is a complete misunderstanding of the threefold order, for that idea embodies the determination to do full justice to those demands that have shown themselves in the unfolding of history. Those demands, three in number, have come to be regarded as party cries, but if we look for their true meaning we shall find that there is an authentic historical impulse contained in them. These three demands contain the impulse of liberty in human life, the impulse towards democracy, and the impulse towards a social form of community.

If these three demands are taken seriously, they cannot be mixed up together under a single administration, because the one must always interfere with the other. If the cry for democracy has any real meaning at all, everyone must acknowledge that it can only flourish in a representative body or parliament, where every single man and woman of full age, being placed on an equality with his fellows, with every other adult in the democratic State, can make decisions from his own judgment.

Now, according to the idea of the threefold membering of the social body, there is a great region of life—that of law and equity, the State and politics—in which every adult has the right, out of his own democratic consciousness, to make himself heard. But if democracy is a reality, and all political life is to be entirely democratized, it is impossible either to include, on the one hand, the cultural life or, on the other, the economic life in the democratic sphere of administration. In the democratic administration a parliament is absolutely in its place, but questions belonging to the department of spiritual life, including education and teaching, can never be properly decided in such a democratic parliament. (I will here only touch upon this subject, as I will deal with it fully in my fourth lecture.) The threefold order strives to realize an independent life of thought, especially in public matters and in everything relating to education and the manner of giving instruction, that is, the State shall no longer determine the matter and manner of teaching.

Only those who are actually teachers, engaged in practical education, shall be its administrators. This means that from the lowest class in the public schools up to the highest grade of education, the teacher shall be independent of any political or economic authority as regards the subject or manner of his teaching. This is a natural consequence of a feeling for what is appropriate to the life of thought within the independent cultural body. The individual need only spend so much time in imparting instruction as will leave him leisure to collaborate in the work of education as a whole and the sphere of spiritual and cultural life in general.

I will try to show in my fourth lecture how this independence of thought places the whole spiritual constitution of man on quite a different footing, and how such independence will bring about precisely what is now believed, because of prevailing prejudice, to be impossible of realization. Through this independence, the life of thought will itself gain strength to take an active and effective part in the life of the state, especially in economic life. Independent thought, far from giving rise to hazy theories or unpractical scientific views, will penetrate into human life, so that out of this independent thought life the individual will permeate himself not with theories, but with knowledge that will fit him to take his place worthily in economic life. Because of its independence, the intellectual life will become practical, so that it may be said that practical and applied knowledge will rule in the cultural sphere. Not that the opinion of every adult person capable of forming a judgment will be authoritative. Parliamentary administration must be deprived of all authority over the cultural body. Whoever believes that it is intended that a democratic parliament should again rule here quite misunderstands the impulse for bringing into existence the social organism consisting of three members.

The same holds good in the economic sphere. The economic life has its own roots and must be governed in accordance with the conditions of its own nature. The manner in which business is carried on cannot be allowed to be judged democratically by every grown-up person, but only by someone who is engaged in some branch of economic life, who is capable in his branch and knows the links that connect his own branch with others. Special knowledge and special capacity are the only guarantees of fruitful work in economic life. Economic life, therefore, will have to be detached from the political and also from the cultural body. It must be placed upon its own basis.

This is just what is most of all misunderstood by socialist thinkers of today. Such thinkers conceive of some form of economic life whereby certain social evils shall cease in the future. We have seen, as it is easy to see, that under the private capitalist order of the last few centuries, certain evils have arisen. The evils are evident enough, but how do people judge them? It is said that it is the private capitalist order that is the cause of these evils; these will disappear as soon as we get rid of the system, when we replace it by the communal system. All the evils that have arisen are caused by the fact that the means of production are in the hands of individual owners. When this private ownership is no longer permitted and the community is in control of the means of production, the evils will cease.

Now it may be said that socialist thinkers have acquired certain isolated facts of knowledge and it is interesting to see how those isolated facts already have their effect in socialist circles. People are saying that the means of production, or capital, which is its equivalent, should be communally administered. We have seen, however, to what state control of certain means of production has led, for instance, of European post offices, European railways, and so forth. We cannot say that the evils have been removed, because the state has become the capitalist. Thus, neither by nationalization nor communalization, nor by the founding of co-operative societies by people who all need the same kind of articles, can any fruitful result be attained. According to the views of socialist thinkers, the people who regulate this consumption, and wish to regulate also the production of the goods to be consumed, become in their turn, as consumers, tyrants over production. The knowledge has, therefore, penetrated the minds of these socialists that nationalization and communalization, as well as the administration by co-operative societies, leads to tyranny on the part of the consumer. The producer would be subjected to the consumer's tyranny. Many therefore think that workers' productive associations in which everybody should have a voice in the management might be founded. In these the workers would unite and produce for themselves according to their own ideas and principles.

Here, again, socialist thinkers have perceived that nothing further would be attained than the replacement of the single capitalist by a number of capitalist working men producers, who would not be able to do otherwise than the private capitalist. Thus, the Worker-Producers' Associations were also cast aside.

But all this fails to convince people that those separate associations cannot lead to fruitful results in the future.

Another scheme was that the whole population of a country, or some particular economic region, might be able to form a great federation in which all the members were to be both producers and consumers, so that no single individual could of his own initiative produce anything for the community. The community itself was to decide how the production should be carried on, how products should be distributed and the like. In short, a great federation embracing production and consumption would be substituted for the private administration now found in our present economic system!

Now anyone with a little insight into facts knows that the idea of founding this great federation in preference to smaller enterprises only arises from the fact that in a larger scheme the errors are less easily detected than in the schemes that propose to nationalize or communalize production and distribution—schemes such as the Worker-Producers' Association and Co-operative Societies. In these latter the field to be surveyed is smaller and the faults committed in founding the enterprises are more easily seen. The great federation embraces a vast social area. Plans are made for the future, and no one sees that the same errors, which were easily discernible in the smaller undertakings, must inevitably again appear. They are not recognized in the larger scheme because in it the promoters are incapable of taking in the whole matter at a glance. This is the explanation. We must understand where the fundamental error in this kind of thought lies, an error leading to the foundation of a great federation in which certain persons presume to take the whole administration of the entire production and consumption into their own hands.

What kind of thought leads to the imagination of such a project? This question can easily be answered if we consult the numerous party programs at the present moment. What gives rise to these party programs? Someone thinks, "Here are certain branches of production; these must be managed by the community; they must then be united in larger branches, in larger administrative districts. Then there must be some kind of central management over the whole, and, above all those, a central board to control the whole consumption and production." What kind of thoughts and representations underlie such an economic scheme as this? Exactly those that are applicable to the political life of modern times. Those who today announce their economic programs have mostly had a purely political training. They have taken part in electioneering campaigns; they know what is expected of them when they are returned to parliament and have to represent their constituents. They are experienced in official and political life. They know the whole routine of political administration and see no reason why it should not be adapted to economic affairs—in a word, economic administration must be altogether modeled on political life.

What we are now so terribly in need of is to see for ourselves that the whole of this routine work, plastered on to the economic system, is something absolutely foreign to its nature. But by far the greater number of persons who now talk of reform, or even of a revolution in economic life, are, as a matter of fact, mere politicians, who persist in thinking that what they have learned in politics can be applied in the management of economic affairs. A healthy condition of the economic system can, however, only prevail if that system be considered by itself and built up out of its own conditions.

What do these political reformers of the economic system want to bring about? They demand nothing less than that this hierarchy of the central management shall determine what is to be produced and how production is to be carried on and the whole manner and process of production brought under the control of the administrative offices. They demand that those persons who are to take part in the work of production shall be engaged and appointed to their places by the central office and that the distribution of raw material to the different works shall be effected by the central office. The entire production would therefore be subject to a kind of hierarchy of political administrators. This is really typical of what is aimed at today in the greater part of the patent schemes for the reform of the economic system. The would-be reformers do not see that these measures would leave the economic system just where it is now; they would not remove its evils; on the contrary, they would immeasurably increase them. The reformers see clearly that nationalization, communalization, co-operative societies, worker-producers' associations, are all alike useless. What they do not see is that by their program they would only transfer to the communal administration of the means of production the very powers to which they object so severely in the private capitalist system.

It is this, above all, that really must be understood today. People must see that such measures and such institutions as those described will of a certainty bring about the conditions we see only too plainly in Eastern Europe today. There, certain individuals were able to carry out these ideas of economic reform and to realize them. People who are willing to learn from facts might see from the fate that threatens Eastern Europe how these measures themselves lead *ad absurdum*. If people were less dogmatic in their ideas and more willing to learn from actual events, nobody would think of saying that the failure of the economic socialization of Hungary was caused by some unimportant factor or other. They would try to find out why it was bound to fail, and then they would be convinced that every such scheme of socialization can only bring destruction and cannot create anything fruitful for the future. But for vast numbers of people it is still difficult to learn from facts in this way. This is best seen in things that are really often treated by socialist thinkers as of secondary importance. They say, it is true, that modern economic life has been transformed by modern technical science, but if they were to carry this train of thought further they would have to recognize the relationship between modern technical science and specialized knowledge and expert skill. They could not help seeing how modern technical science everywhere intervenes in industrialism, but they refuse to see it. So they say, in parentheses, they will have nothing to do with technical science in the processes of production. It can take care of itself. They only wish to occupy themselves with the manner in which those who are engaged in production processes live socially, what sort of social life they lead.

If people will only open their eyes to facts, nothing can be more evident than the immense importance of the part directly played by technical science in economic affairs. One example, a really typical one, may be given here. By multiplying machines, technical science has, to put it in a few words, succeeded in providing commodities for public consumption. To the existence of this machinery the fact is due that from four hundred to five hundred millions of tons of coal were brought to the surface per annum for industrial purposes before the War. Now if one calculates the amount of economic energy and power required by those machines, which are entirely the result of human thought and can only be worked by human thought, the following interesting result is arrived at. If we reckon an eight-hour day, we get the startling result that by these machines, that is, through the human thought incorporated in the machines, through the inventive gift of the mind, as much energy and working force are used as could be produced by seven to eight hundred millions of men!

Hence, if you picture to yourself that the earth has a working population of about 1500 million men, it has gained, by the inventive genius of human beings in the recent periods of modern civilization, seven hundred to eight hundred millions more. Therefore, two thousand millions of human beings work, that is to say, while the seven to eight hundred millions do not themselves actually work, but the machines work for them. What works in these machines? The human intellect.

It is of the utmost significance that facts like these, which might easily be multiplied, should be grasped because they show that technical science cannot be treated with indifference and lightly put aside. Rather, it co-operates actively and ceaselessly in industrial life and is inseparable from it. Modern economic life is altogether unthinkable without the basis of modern technical science and without special knowledge and expert skill.

To overlook these things is to set out with preconceived ideas, inspired by human passions, and to close our eyes to realities. The idea of the threefold order of the social body is honest in its endeavors to solve the social problem. For that reason its standpoint cannot be the same as that of party leaders, with catchwords and programs. The Threefold Order must start from facts. Hence, taking its stand on the realities of life, it must recognize that industry, especially in our complicated life, is based on the initiative of the individual. If we try to substitute for individual initiative the abstract community at large, we give the death-blow to economic life. Eastern Europe will prove this, if it remains much longer under its present rule. It means extinction and death to the economic body when we deprive the individual of his initiative, which must proceed from his intellect and take part in the ordering of the means of production purely for the benefit of human society.

What is the origin of the evils we see today? The modern process of production, because of its technical perfection, necessitates the initiative of the individual and therefore necessitates that the individual shall have capital at his disposal, and that he shall be able to carry on production on his own initiative—these are the results of the recent development of humanity. The accompanying evils, as

36

we shall see, grow out of different causes. If we want to know their origin, we must, in the first place, take our stand, not on the company principle, not even on the great syndicate principle, but we must take our stand on the principle of association.

What do we mean by taking our stand on the principle of association rather than on that of companies? We mean that whoever takes his stand on the company principle considers that all that is necessary is for individuals to join together, to confer together, and come to resolutions; then they can control the process of production. Thus the first thing is to join together, and form the company; then from this society, from this community of human beings, to start production. The idea of the threefold social organism starts from realities. It requires, in the first place, that men should be there who can produce, who have technical knowledge and special skill. On them must depend the business of production. These experts in technical knowledge and skill must unite and carry on the economic activity founded on the production that springs from individual initiative. This is the true principle of association. Commodities are first produced and then brought to the consumer on the basis of the union of the producers.

What may be called the misfortune of our age is that the difference, the radical difference between these two principles is not understood because, as a matter of fact, everything depends on their being understood. The instinct to observe that every abstract community that attempts to control production must undermine the process is entirely wanting. The associative community can only receive what is produced by the initiative of the individual who offers it to the community, to the consumer.

The most important aspect of these things is not perceived for the reason I gave yesterday. I said then that at about the time of the

Renaissance, of the Reformation, at the beginning of modern history, the precious metals began to be introduced into Europe from Central and South America, and that this led to the substitution of the financial for the natural system of economy, up till then almost the only prevailing system. By this change, a significant economic revolution was accomplished in Europe. Conditions then arose that still influence us today. These conditions have at the same time shut out the view like a curtain that prevents one from obtaining sight of true realities.

Let us look more closely at these conditions. Let us begin with the old system of natural economy, though it is not so much in evidence in our day. The only factor in that economic process is the commodity produced by the individual. This he can exchange for something produced by another. In this natural economic system, according to which one product is exchanged for another, a certain standard of quality must be attained since, if I wish to barter one commodity for another, I must have something that I can exchange for it that the other accepts as of equal value. This means that people are forced to produce if they want anything. They are forced to exchange something that has a real, an obviously real, value. In place of this exchange of commodities that have a real value in human life, we have introduced finance, and money has become the medium with which one buys and sells, as one buys and sells with real objects in the natural economic system. We need only recall the fact that money, by becoming a real object in economic transactions, deludes men as to its true nature and, by producing this imaginary effect, at the same time tyrannizes over them.

Take an extreme case. Let us assume that the credit system I mentioned at the close of my lecture yesterday, makes its way into the economy of finance. As a matter of fact, it has done so of late in many cases. The following example shows the result of this. A government or an individual enterprise wants to install a telegraph system. A considerable amount of credit can be raised and the scheme is successfully carried out. Certain circumstances demand considerable amounts of money, and interest on these amounts must be paid; provision must be made for the payment of interest. What do we find in many instances within our social structure especially when the state itself does this business? It happens most frequently in state enterprises that the object for which the money was provided and employed has long since become useless; it is no longer there but the public funds still go on paying off what was once demanded as credit. In other words, the object for which the debt was incurred has vanished, but the money is still an object of economic transaction. Such things have a world economic significance. Napoleon III, who was completely under the spell of modern ideas, took it into his head to embellish Paris and he had many buildings erected. The ministers who were his willing tools carried out the operations. It occurred to them that the national income might be applied to pay the interest. The result is that Paris has been much improved, but the people are still paying the old debt. That is to say, long after the thing has ceased to have any real foundation, manipulations are still going on with the money that has itself become an economic object.

This had, to be sure, its advantages. When business was carried on in the old natural system of economy, the production of commodities was necessary. These were, of course, liable to spoilage, and people had to work, and to continue working, so as to keep up a supply of goods. This is not necessary with money. A man gives over money, lends it, insures himself; that is, money transactions are carried on quite independently of those who produce commodities.

Money emancipates man in a certain sense from the actual economic process, just because it becomes itself an economic process. This is extremely significant. In the old natural economy, one individual depended on another. Men were forced to work together, to bear with one another. They had to agree on certain arrangements, otherwise the economic life could not go on. Under the financial system the capitalist is, of course, also dependent on those who work, but he is quite a stranger to these workers. How close was the tie between consumer and producer in the old natural economy in which actual commodities were dealt with! How remote is the person who transacts business in money from those who work in order that his money may yield interest! A deep gulf has opened between one human being and another. They do not get near to each other under the financial system of economy. This is one of the first things to be considered if we wish to understand how the masses of workers (no matter whether they are intellectual or manual workers) can again be brought together with those who also make business possible by lending capital. This, however, can only be done through the principle of association, by which men will again unite with each other as men. The principle of association is a demand of social life, but a demand such as I have described it, not one resembling those that often figure in socialistic programs.

What else has happened under the ever-increasing influence of modern finance? What is called human labor has become dependent upon it. The regulating of human labor in the social structure is a subject of dispute among socialists themselves, and excellent grounds can be found for and against what is said on both sides. One can understand—especially when one has learned not to think and feel *about* the proletariat, but to think and feel *with* the proletariat—one can well understand why the proletarian says that his labor power must no longer be a commodity. It must no longer be possible that commodities are bought on the market, and human labor is also bought on the labor market and paid for in the form of wages.

That is easy to understand. It is also easy to understand that Karl Marx had many followers when he calculated that the workman produces a profit and that he is not paid the full value of his labor, but that the profit produced by him goes to the employer. It is easy to understand that under the influence of such a theory, the workman should fight about this profit. It is just as easy to prove that wages are paid out of capital, and that modern economic life is altogether regulated by capitalism, that certain products create capital and, according to the capital created, wages are paid, labor purchased. That means wages are produced by capital. One argument can be proved as clearly as the other. It can be proved that capital is the parasite of labor; it can also be proved that wages are created by capital. In short, the opinions of either party may be defended with the same validity. This fact ought to be once for all thoroughly grasped. Then it will be understood why it is that, today, when people seek to attain something, they do so preferably by fighting for it, not by progressive thought and by accounting for circumstances. Work is by its nature so entirely different from commodities that it is quite impossible to pay money in the same way for goods and labor without economic injury, but people do not understand the difference. They still do not see through the economic structure, especially in this section of it. There are countless economists in our day who say, "If money, the currency, either coin or paper money, is increased *ad lib.*, it loses its value, and the necessaries of life, especially the most indispensable, go up in price." We observe this and see the folly of simply increasing the currency, for the mere increase, as anyone can see, has only the effect of raising the price of the necessaries of life. The well-known endless screw is still turning!

There is another thing that is not understood. As soon as labor is paid for in the same way as commodities or products, it must happen as a matter of course that at that moment labor begins to fight for better and better pay, for higher and higher wages. But the money that labor receives as wages plays the same part in the determining of prices as the mere increase of the money in circulation. This ought to be understood. You may do as many a minister of finance has done and, instead of increasing production and taking care to improve it, you may simply issue banknotes and increase the currency. Then there will be more money in circulation, but all commodities, especially those indispensable to life, will be dearer. People see this for themselves; therefore they see how foolish it is simply to increase the money in circulation. What they do not see is that all the money that is spent in order to pay labor actually has the effect of raising the price of commodities because sound prices can only be fixed within an independent economic system. Sound prices can only be fixed when they develop in accordance with the true valuation of human activity. Therefore the idea of the threefold order of the social organism is to detach labor completely from the economic process. It will be my task especially tomorrow to go into this matter in detail.

Labor as labor has no place in the economic process. It may seem strange, or even paradoxical, to say what I am about to say, but many things now seem paradoxical that we must nevertheless understand. Consider how far people have fallen away from right thinking! For this reason they often find things absurd that must,

42

nevertheless, be said because they are true. Let us suppose that a man gives himself up to sport from morning till evening, that he makes it his occupation. He expends exactly the same labor-force as one who chops wood, and in exactly the same manner. What is important is to use one's strength in working for the community at large. The sportsman does not do this; the most that can be said of him is that he makes himself strong, only, as a rule, he does not turn his strength to account. Generally, it is of no importance to the community that a man make a profession of sport by which he tires himself as much as by chopping wood. Chopping wood is of some use. That is to say, the use of labor-power has no importance socially, but what results from such use has a meaning in social life. We must look at the result of the application of labor. That is valuable to the community. Hence, the only thing that can be of value in economic life is the product of labor-power, and the only thing with which the administration of economic life can have any concern is the regulation of the comparative values of products. Labor must lie quite outside the economic circuit. It belongs to the department of equity, of which we shall speak tomorrow, in which every adult human being has a right to make himself heard, on equal terms with every other human being. The manner and duration and the kind of work will be determined by the legal conditions prevailing between man and man. Labor must be lifted out of the economic process. Then there will remain to be regulated by the economic system only the valuation of commodities and of the service that one person should receive from another in exchange for his own service. For this purpose certain persons will withdraw from the associations composed of producers of various things, or of producers and consumers, and so on. These people will occupy themselves with the fixing of prices. Labor will lie entirely outside the sphere to be regulated in the economic process; it will be banished from it. As long as labor is within the economic system, it must be paid out of capital. This is precisely the cause of all that we call striving for mere profit, the race for wealth in modern times because in this process the man who has commodities to supply is himself part of the process that ends at last in the market. At this point it is important that a highly erroneous idea should be corrected by all who wish to see things in their true light. We say the capitalist places his commodities on the market to make a profit from them. For a long time socialist thinkers have been saying with a considerable amount of justice that the moral law has nothing whatever to do with this production, but that only economic thought is concerned with it. Today, however, a great deal is said from the ethical standpoint on the subject of profit and gain. Here we are going to speak neither from an ethical, nor from a merely economic point of view; we speak from the point of view of the whole of human society. The question must be asked, "What is it that arises as gain, or profit?" It is something that plays the same role in social economy that the rising quicksilver plays in the tube of the thermometer. The rising of the quicksilver shows that the temperature has risen. We know that it is not the quicksilver that has made the room warmer, but that the increased warmth is caused by other factors. The market profit resulting from present conditions of production is only a sign that commodities can be produced that yield a profit. Otherwise, I should like to know how anyone can possibly discover whether a commodity ought to be produced if not from the fact that, when it has been produced and placed on the market, it yields a profit. This is the only sign showing that one may influence the economic system by bringing out this product. The only way in which we know whether or not a commodity should be produced is

44

that it finds a sale when placed on the market. If there is no demand for it, there is no profit in it.

These are the facts, without all the rambling talk about demand and supply that we find in the theories of so many economists. The consideration that lies at the root of the matter in this sphere is that the yielding of profit is at present the one and only thing enabling a man to produce a certain commodity, because it will have a certain value in the community. The remodeling of the market, which today operates in this way, will follow as soon as a real principle of association finds a place in our social life. Then it will no longer be the impersonal supply and demand having nothing to do with the human being that will determine whether a commodity shall be produced or not. Then, from those associations, by the will of those working in them, other persons will be brought in whose business it will be to find the relation between the value of a manufactured commodity and its price. We may say that the value of a commodity does not come under consideration. It certainly gives the impulse to the demand, but the demand in our present social conditions is extremely doubtful because there is always the question whether there are sufficient means available to make the demand possible. We may want things; if we do not possess the means to satisfy our wants, we shall not be able to create a demand. What is essential is that a connecting link be formed between human needs, which give the commodities their value, and the value itself because the commodity we need acquires its human value always in accordance with that need. Institutions must arise out of the social order that form a link between the value attached to the commodities by human needs, and the right prices. The prices are now fixed by the market in accordance with the known purchasing power of potential buyers. A truly social order must be guided by the fact that those

45

who quite justifiably must have commodities must be able to pay for them, that is, the prices must fit the value of the commodities and correspond to it. Instead of the present chaotic market, there must be an arrangement by which the tyrannizing over human needs and the interference with consumption is eradicated. The methods of the Worker-Producers' Associations and the Co-operative Societies must cease, research be made into the scope of consumption, and decisions reached on how consumption needs can be met.

For this purpose, and following the principle of association, it will be possible to produce a supply of commodities corresponding to the needs that have been investigated. That is, arrangements must exist with persons who can study the wants of consumers. Statistics can only give the present state of affairs. They can never be authoritative about the future. The needs for the time being must be studied, and, in accordance with these, measures must be taken to produce what is needed. When a product shows a tendency to become too dear, that is a sign that there are too few workers engaged on it. Negotiations must then be carried on with other branches of production to transfer workers from one branch to another where the need lies, in order that more of the lacking products may be supplied. If a commodity tends to become too cheap, that is to say, to earn too little profit, arrangements must be made to employ fewer workers on that particular product. This means that in the future the satisfaction of the needs of the community will depend on the way in which men are employed in industry. The price of the product is conditional on the number of persons engaged in its production. But, through these arrangements, the price will really correspond to the value attached to the commodity in question by the community in accordance with its requirements.

46

So we see that human reason will take the place of chance, that as the result of the arrangements that will come into existence the price will express the agreements arrived at, the contracts entered into. Thus we shall see a revolution of the market accomplished by the substitution of reason for the chances of the market now prevailing.

We see, then, that as soon as we detach the economic body from the two other departments, which we shall discuss in the following lectures when we shall also treat of the relationship of the other departments to the economic body and of many things which must now seem difficult to understand—as soon as the economic body has been detached from the two others, the State or rights body and the spiritual or cultural body, the economic body will find itself on a sound and reasonable basis because the only thing with which it will have to concern itself will be the manner of carrying on business. It will no longer be necessary to influence the prices of commodities by manipulating them so that these prices will determine how long or how much the people should work and what wages should be paid, and so on. The only thing that need be considered in economic life will be the relative values of commodities. In this way economic life will be placed on a sound basis, and this sound basis must be preserved for the whole economic life. Hence, in such an economic life as this there will be a return to a condition that has now almost ceased to exist because of the financial system in which money itself has become an object of economic business, a condition in which economic life will be re-established on its natural and worthy foundation. It will not be possible in future to carry on business by means of money and for money because economic institutions will have to deal with the respective values of the commodities. That is to say, society will again return to goodness of quality, excellence of workmanship and the capability of the worker. The granting of credit will no longer depend on the condition that money is available or tight, or on the degree of the risk to be taken; it will depend entirely upon the existence of men capable of starting an enterprise or of producing something. Human ability will command credit. Since human capability will condition the amount of credit to be granted, that amount can never be given in excess of human capability. If you merely give money and allow it to be used, the object to which it has been applied may long have ceased to exist, but the money is still the object of transactions. If the money is given for human capability, when that human capability comes to an end the object for which the money is used also ceases to exist. We shall discuss this in the following lectures. Not until the economic body is supported by the two other departments of social life, the independent political and the independent cultural body, not until then can the economic system be established independently in a sound way on its own foundation. To this end, everything within the economic system must grow out of the conditions proper to itself. Material commodities are produced out of these conditions. We need only think of an instance in social life, of something that might be compared to a waste product of economic life, and we shall see how, as a result of true economic thinking, many things must be discarded that are now reckoned as a matter of course in the social order and are even defended as progressive measures of social science.

Among all those who today profess to be experts in practical life, there is not a single individual who doubts that an improvement has been made by the transition from all kinds of indirect taxation and other sources of national income to what we call the income tax, especially the graduated income tax. Everyone thinks it is unquestionably right to pay income tax and yet, however paradoxical this may sound to the modern mind, the belief that the imposition of a tax on income is a just measure is only an illusion resulting from the modern financial system of economy. We earn money; we trade with it. By money we detach ourselves from the sound productive process itself. Money is made into an abstraction, so to speak, in the economic process, just as thoughts are in the process of thought. Just as it is impossible to call up by enchantment real ideas and feelings from abstract thought, so it is likewise impossible to bring forth by enchantment something real from money, if that money is not merely a symbol for commodities that are produced, if it is not merely a kind of bookkeeping, a currency system of bookkeeping, in which every piece of money must represent a commodity. This subject will also be more fully discussed in the following lectures. Today it must be stated that in a period that is only concerned with turning money into an economic object, incomes cannot escape being considered an object of taxation.

By imposing taxes we make ourselves co-responsible with others for the whole system of financial economy. Something is taxed that is not a commodity at all, but only a symbol for a commodity. We are dealing with an abstraction from the economic life. Money only becomes a reality when it is spent for something. It then takes its place in the circuit of economic life, whether I spent it on amusement, or for bodily or mental necessities, or whether I bank it to be used in the economic process. Banking my money is a way of spending it. This must, of course, be kept in mind. Money becomes a reality in the economic process at the moment it passes out of my possession into the process of economic life. If people would reflect, they would see that it is of no use for a man to have a large income. If he hoards it, it may be his, but it is of no use in the economic

49

process. The only thing that benefits a person is the ability to spend a great deal. In public life today, in a life fruitful of results, the ability to spend a great deal is just the sign of a large income. Hence, if a system of taxation is to be created that constitutes a real service of the economic process to the good of the general community, instead of a parasitical growth upon it, capital must be taxed at the moment it is transferred to the economic process. Strange to relate, income tax comes to be transformed into a tax on expenditure, which I beg you not to confound with indirect taxation. Indirect taxation is often the expression of the wishes of rulers at the present day, because the direct taxes and income tax do not ordinarily yield enough. We are not referring to either direct or indirect taxation in speaking of the tax on expenditure; the point in question is that at the moment my capital passes into the economic process and becomes productive, it shall be taxed.

Precisely by this example of taxation, we see how necessary is a change in our method of thinking, and how the belief that a tax on income is first in importance is an accompaniment of that financial system that has appeared in modern civilization since the Renaissance and Reformation. When the economic system is once placed upon its own basis, the only matter to be considered is that capital actually involved in the production of commodities shall supply the means for the manufacture of the products necessary to the community. It will then be a case of a tax on expenditure, but never one on income.

These are things we must relearn, and we must change our method of thinking. In these two lectures I have only been able to give a sketch of the matter with which I shall deal much more exhaustively in the next four lectures. Anyone who gives utterance to such things knows well that he will arouse opposition on all sides, that at first hardly anyone will agree with him because all such matters are overlaid by party opinion. No improvement can be hoped for, however, until they are raised out of the sphere of party passions into that of true thought resulting from close connection with life. How desirable it would be if people, on first hearing of the three-membered social organism, instead of judging in accordance with their party programs and opinions, would take their own instinct for truth to aid them in forming their judgments. Party opinions and principles have in many cases led people away from that feeling for truth. Hence, one finds over and over again that those who are more or less dependent on the mere consumption of commodities really find it easy, prompted by their own feeling for the truth, to understand what is the aim of such an institution as the three-membered social organism. But then come the leaders, especially those of the masses of the socialist party, and it cannot be denied that the leaders show no inclination to enter into consideration of reality. One thing belonging more especially to economic life is unfortunately evident, and this is one of the most urgent matters of the social question.

I found, when speaking to the workers on the threefold order, that their own instinct for truth enabled them to understand well what was said. Then came the leaders who told them that what was proposed was only a utopia. It certainly did not agree with their own thoughts or with all that had been working in their brains for decades. They told their faithful followers that these were utopian ideas, without reality. Unfortunately, blind faith has grown too strong in modern times, a blind following, a terrible feeling of subjection to authority in these circles. It must be said that all the respect for authority once shown to bishops and archbishops of the Catholic Church is nothing as compared with that shown by the masses of modern workers to their leaders. This makes it comparatively easy for those leaders to carry out their intentions. What I wish to do is to point out above all things what is honest and not what merely serves cut and dried party interest. If I should be able to succeed in these lectures in showing that what is sought for in the threefold organism is really honestly intended for the general welfare of all humanity, without distinction of class, conditions, and so forth, the main object of these lectures will have been achieved.

III

LEGAL QUESTIONS.
THE TASK AND THE LIMITATIONS OF DEMOCRACY.
PUBLIC LAW. CRIMINAL LAW.

The acquisition of right views on social life depends to a large extent on a clear understanding of the relations existing between human beings who, in their life together, organize the social conditions and the institutions under which they live. An unprejudiced onlooker will discover that all the institutions in social life originate in the first place from measures dictated by the will of man. He who has won his way to this view will come to the conclusion that the factor of decisive importance in social life is the conduct of human beings towards each other, the employment of their forces, their capacities and their feelings towards others in a social or unsocial manner. People imbued with social sentiments and views will mold their institutions so as to make them work socially. It is true to a great extent that the ability or inability of any individual to provide himself with the necessities of life out of his income will depend on the manner in which his fellow creatures furnish him with the means of a livelihood, upon whether they work for him in such a way that he can support himself out of his own means. To put this in the most practical form, the ability of man to procure enough bread for his wants will depend upon the fact that society has taken the needful steps to enable everyone who works, or who performs a service, to have a corresponding quantity of bread in return for his work. The opportunity of really turning his work to account, of bringing it to that point at which he can earn what he needs for his existence, is again determined by the presence of social institutions in his environment, by the aid of which he can find his proper place.

Now it really requires only a small amount of unprejudiced insight into social life in order to recognize what has just been said is an axiom, a fundamental principle of the social question. Whoever does not recognize it will hardly acknowledge the truth of the principle, because he has no inclination to look at life with an unprejudiced mind in order to convince himself, as he might from every occurrence in life, that it is so. It is true that this way of viewing life is particularly unpleasant for the average man, for it is a matter of great importance to him that he should be left undisturbed. He is willing to hear of institutions being improved and transformed into something better, but he regards it as an infringement of his dignity as a man if it is found necessary to tell him that he ought to change his own outlook on life and his own manner of living. He gladly agrees that institutions should be modeled on social lines. He is not at all pleased, however, with the proposal that he should model his own conduct on these lines. Hence, something most remarkable has entered into the modern history of evolution. In the course of the last few centuries, as I have already shown in the first lecture, economic life has developed far beyond all the conceptions that have been formed of it, especially in the spheres of law and of cultural life. I pointed out in the first lecture that the social criticism of Woodrow Wilson himself amounted to nothing more or less than the statement that the economic system has laid down the law: "Economic life has made its demands; it has been advancing, and has assumed certain distinct forms. The legal system and cultural life, through which we seek to govern the economic system, have remained stationary at their old points of view. They have not kept pace." In these sentiments Woodrow Wilson has undoubtedly expressed a deeply significant fact of modern evolution.

With the rise of the complicated conditions of technical industry and of the equally complicated capitalist conditions entailed by the former, with the era of big industrial enterprises, economic life has simultaneously put forward its demands. The facts of economic life have gradually eluded us. They go their own way more or less. We have not found the force within ourselves to govern economic life by our thoughts and ideas.

Modern thought regarding the demands of economic life, the consideration of economic matters, as these come under direct observation, have led more and more to adaptation of legal and intellectual conceptions to these immediate facts. Thus we may say that the chief characteristic in the evolution of humanity for centuries has been that the conceptions of law, according to which men strive to live at peace with one another, as well as those of intellectual or spiritual life, according to which they develop and form their capacities, have become to a great extent dependent on economic life. The extent to which in modern times human thought, and the attitude of human beings towards one another, have become dependent on economic matters passes quite unnoticed. Of course, the institutions of the last centuries have been created by human beings themselves, but for the most part they are not based upon new thoughts and ideas; they are, rather, the outcome of unconscious impulses and unconscious instincts. In this way something we may truly call an element of anarchy has arisen in the structure of the social organism. In the first two lectures of this series, I have described from different points of view this element of anarchy in the social organism. But within this social edifice of modern times, those conditions have arisen that have led to the modern form of the proletarian question. To the workman, called away from his handicraft and placed at the machine, shut up in the factory, what was the most obvious fact as he looked at life around him? Looking at his own life he saw chiefly that all his thoughts, all his rights with regard to other men, in fact, everything is determined by powerful economic conditions, by those economic conditions that he must accept because he is economically weak as against the economically strong. Thus it may be said that in the leading circles, among the governing classes, there is an unconscious denial of the fundamental principle that human institutions should grow out of the conscious life of men themselves. People have forgotten to apply this truth in social life. Gradually these leading, governing classes have given themselves up instinctively to a life in which culture and law are subject to the power of the economic system, even though they may not believe this. This has given rise to a dogmatic conception of life among socialist thinkers and their followers. The conception of life that has resulted from this thought is that such conditions are inevitable in human evolution, that there is no possibility for the individual person to organize legal conditions or a system of culture suitable to himself. They believe that culture and law result naturally as appendages to economic realities, to branches of production and so on.

Thus among large numbers of people the social question has

adopted as its starting-point a positive demand. Their fundamental belief was that the economic system conditions the life of rights, conditions too, the cultural life of the people. Therefore the economic life must be reformed so as to bring forth a system of laws and culture corresponding to the needs and demands of the masses. The proletariat has learnt from the life and habits of the leading classes to believe consciously what the latter had carried out instinctively in their lives; it made this a dogma. Today the social question faces us in the following aspect. Among great masses of people there is a widespread conviction that, if only the economic life and institutions were revolutionized, everything else, law and culture, would evolve of themselves; that economically just, good, socially organized legal and cultural institutions would result. Under the influence of this opinion they have failed to recognize the real crux of the modern social problem. The point on which the whole social question turns has been hidden by this dogma through a great deception, a mighty illusion. The fact is that precisely these conditions—the dependence of law and culture on the economic life—are a historical result of evolution. This must be overcome. While in wide socialist circles the belief is current that the economic system must first be changed and everything else will follow of itself, the truth is that each one must ask himself the question: What conditions within the sphere of equity and of culture must first be created in order that a new cultural and a new legal system may give birth to economic conditions that will satisfy the demands of an existence worthy of human beings? Not the question: How can we bring law and culture gradually into dependence on the economic life? But rather: How can we escape from that dependence? That is the question to be asked before any other.

This is an important consideration because it shows us the obstacle barring an unprejudiced understanding of the present social question. It shows us that one of the chief obstacles is a dogma that has grown up in the course of centuries. This dogma has become so firmly fixed that at present countless educated and uneducated persons of proletarian and other classes ridicule the idea that the system of equity and of culture could be purified in any other way than by the reformation of the economic system itself.

It is my task today to speak of the equity state; the day after tomorrow I will speak of the cultural life. The equity state, due to its particular nature and significance, has often presented to us the question: What is really the origin of rights? What is the origin of that feeling that prompts men to say in their dealings with one another that a thing is just or unjust? This question has always been an extremely important one. Yet it is a strange fact that many social thinkers have entirely lost sight of the actual question of rights. It no longer exists for them. There are certainly many academic-theoretical treatises extant regarding the nature and meaning of law, but what is generally characteristic in the study of social matters is that the question of equity is more or less neglected.

In dealing with this subject, I must call your attention to something that at the present time is becoming more and more evident, although a short time ago it was quite unobserved. People have become aware of the approach of untenable social conditions. Even those whose own lives have remained more or less untouched by the present unsocial conditions have attempted to find a solution. Though a comparatively short time ago people laughed at the idea of legal and cultural spheres influencing economic affairs, today we encounter ever more frequently the assertion that seems to come from the obscure depths of consciousness. It is quite true that in the relationships of human beings in social life, questions affecting the feelings and relating to equity must also be taken into account. Much of the confusion in social conditions has been caused by the want of consideration given to moral and psychic relationships and to conditions of equity on their own ground. Thus there is now a slight indication—so obvious that it can no longer be overlooked—that an improvement in the present conditions must come from a quarter different from that of purely economic interests. But this has as yet little influence on the practical discussion of the question.

Like a crimson thread running through all the sentiments of the later socialist thinkers is the belief that a social structure must be built up in which human beings can live in accordance with their capacities and needs. Whether these sentiments are developed in the direction of extreme radicalism, or incline more to conservative thought, is not the point. We hear on all sides that the evils of the existing social order are due, in large measure, to the fact that within that order a man is not in a position to use his full capacities. On the other hand we hear that the social order must be so constituted that he can satisfy his wants within its limits.

Here we are brought back to two fundamental elements of human life. Capacities belong to the human power of imagination because, since a man must act consciously, his capacities in the first instance arise out of his power of imagination, his thought-will. Of course, the power of imagination must be continually fired and filled with enthusiasm, by feeling, but feeling alone is powerless if the fundamental imagination is absent. Therefore, the question of a man's efficiency or practical skill brings us in the last instance to the life of imagination. It became evident to many persons that care must be taken to enable a man to realize in social life his power of imagination. The other element that has to be allowed free play has more to do with the will in man. Will power, which is connected with desire, the craving for something or other, is a fundamental force in the human being. When it is said that the human being must live within a social structure that can satisfy his wants, it is the will that is under consideration.

Thus, unknown to themselves, even the Marxists, in advancing their social theories, consider human beings while they profess to speak only of institutions. They speak of institutions, but they would like to make their institutions such that human ideas and human faculties find scope within them, and that human needs can be satisfied for all alike as they arise.

Now there is something peculiar in this view. It leaves out of account one element of human life, and that is the life of feeling. If we put forward a claim to build up a social edifice in which people can live in accordance with their capacities, their feelings and their needs, then we are taking into consideration the whole man. Curiously enough, although the Marxist theory enters into details as to social aims, it characteristically omits the life of feeling altogether. To omit feeling in the study of human nature is to leave out all consideration of the actual conditions of equity in the social organism. For conditions of equity can only develop in a community of human beings in accordance with the feelings that have been trained and refined. As people feel towards each other in their mutual intercourse, so will be the system of public law. Because of the omission of this vital element of feeling in the consideration of the social question the problem of equity was necessarily lost sight of. It is, however, essential that this matter of law should be placed in the proper light. Of course we know that law exists, but the desire exists also to represent it as a mere dependent of the economic system.

In what manner is law developed in a community? Attempts have often been made to give a definition of law, but a satisfactory one has not yet been found. Just as little has resulted from the attempt to trace the origin of law, to discover whence it comes. A solution of this problem has been sought in vain. Why is this so? It resembles what would result from an effort to develop language out of human nature alone. It has often been said, and rightly, that a person who grew up on a desert island would never learn to speak because speech is acquired through communion with other beings within the whole human family.

Likewise, out of the interchange of human feelings in public life the desire for law is kindled. We cannot say that the feeling for justice suddenly awakens in some particular part of the human being, or of the human race. We may say that the feelings human beings mutually develop in their intercourse with one another bring them into certain relationships, and as these relationships express themselves, laws are established. Thus we discover law as a development within, and out of, human society. Herewith we come right up against what has developed in modern history as the demands of democracy. We cannot understand the nature of the democratic demands unless we look at human evolution itself as a kind of organism. But the modern method of study is far removed from this manner of considering the question. No one would deny that it is reasonable to ask what the cause is of those forces in human nature that bring about the change of teeth in the child about the seventh year. It is not reasonable to look for the cause of this process in the kind of nourishment the child is fed—whether it be beef or cabbage. In like manner we must ask what the cause is of the development in the human organism that is manifested at the age of puberty. We must look at the inner nature of what develops. Search as you may among modes of thought today, you will find none that can apply this method to the history of human evolution. None, for instance, is clear on this point, namely, that in the course of the development of humanity on earth certain powers and capacities, certain attributes developed in the succeeding epochs of time out of the inner nature of the human being himself. He who learns to study nature in accordance with its own laws can transfer this method of observation to the study of history. If this method be followed, it will be found that since the middle of the fifteenth century the longing for democracy, more or less fulfilled in the various regions of the earth, has been growing out of the depths of human nature. This longing is expressed in the demand that in social life the human being can recognize as valid for others only what he feels to be right and best for himself. In modern times the democratic principle has become the sign and seal of human social endeavor and has grown out of the depths of human nature. The demand of modern humanity for this principle of democracy is an elemental force. He who has an insight into these matters must treat them with the greatest seriousness. He must ask himself what the significance and limitations of the democratic principle are. I have just defined this principle. It consists in the fact that the persons forming a definite social organism adopt resolutions approved by every individual within the community. These resolutions, of course, can only be binding if they are adopted by a majority. The content of such majority resolutions is democratic only if every single individual is on an equal basis with every other single individual. These resolutions can only be adopted on any matter when every single individual is in reality the equal of every other. That is, democratic resolutions can only be passed when every adult is entitled to vote because he is an adult and therefore capable of judging.

Herewith we have defined the limitations of democracy as clearly as possible. On the basis of democracy only such things can be determined as are capable of determination through the fact that a person has reached the years of discretion. All such things as are related to the development of human capacity in public life are excluded from democratic measures. Everything in the nature of education and instruction, of cultural life in general, requires the devotion of the individual human being—in the next lecture this will be more fully dealt with—it demands, above all things, real individual understanding of the human being, special individual capacities in the teacher, in the educator, which by no means belong to a person merely because he is an adult. We must either not take democracy seriously, in which case we submit to its decisions regarding human capacities, or we do take democracy seriously, and then we must exclude from it the administration of the cultural life and the economic life. Everything that I described yesterday in regard to the economic sphere is based on the assumption that individuals actively engaged in one or another special branch are possessed of expert knowledge and efficiency. For instance, mere maturity in age, the mere capacity of judgment possessed by every adult, can never be sufficient qualification for a good farmer or a good industrial worker. Hence, majority resolutions must be kept out of the realm of economic life. The same applies to the cultural life. Thus there arises between these two realms the actual democratic state-life in which every individual confronts every other as competent to form a judgment, because he is of full age and all are equal as human beings, but in which majority resolutions can be carried only on matters dependent on the same capacity of judgment in all adult persons. If we take the trouble to test the truth of these things by the facts of life and not regard them as mere abstractions, we shall see that people deceive themselves, because these are difficult thoughts and because they have not the courage actually to follow up these ideas to their logical conclusion. But the unwillingness to do so and the substitution of different things for the universal demand of democracy have had, in the evolution of modern humanity, a concrete significance. I will exemplify these matters from the historical evolution of mankind itself rather than from abstract principles.

During recent years we have witnessed the collapse of a state. We have seen it fall to pieces of itself, we might say, and this state may really serve as an object of experiment in regard to the question of rights and law. It is the old Austria-Hungary, which no longer exists. Anyone who has followed the events of recent war years knows that at the end the downfall of Austria was brought about by purely military events, but the dissolution of the Austrian State, which followed in the second place, was the result of its inner conditions. This State collapsed and would probably have done so even had the military events in Austria been more creditable. This may be said of the events in Austria by one who has had the opportunity (I have spent thirty years of my life in that country) of following consecutively for decades the conditions there. It was in the 'sixties' of last century that the demand for democracy, that is, for a representative government, arose in Austria. Now how was this representation of the people composed? The representatives of the people in the Austrian Imperial Parliament were recruited from four purely economic sections: 1. The great landowners; 2. The towns, market and industrial centers; 3. Chambers of Commerce; 4. Provincial Councils. But in these last only economic interests were actually represented. Therefore, according to the section to which one belonged, province, or Chamber of Commerce, one voted for the representatives in the Austrian Imperial Parliament. Thus representatives of purely economic interests sat in that Parliament. The resolutions adopted by them were, of course, arrived at by a majority of individual men, but these individuals represented interests that arose out of their identification with the great land-owning class, with the towns, markets and industrial centers, with the Chambers of Commerce or the Provincial Councils. What kind of public measures were adopted by the decisions of a majority? They were legal measures, the result of deliberations by nothing but economic interests in disguise, for when, for instance, the Chambers of Commerce were unanimous with the great landowners about anything that benefited them economically, a majority could be found to vote against the interests of the minority, who were, perhaps, just those most concerned in the matter. When parliaments are composed of representatives of economic interests, majorities can always be found to pass resolutions affecting those interests and to make laws that have nothing whatever to do with that feeling for justice that exists between one man and another.

Or let us call to mind that in the old German Imperial Parliament there is a great party, calling itself the Center, representing purely cultural interests, that is, Roman Catholic cultural interests. This party can join with any other in order to gain a majority, and the result is that purely cultural needs are satisfied by the enactment of public laws. It happened countless numbers of times. This peculiarity of the modern parliament, which passes for a democratic institution, has often been commented on, but no one has discovered how it might be altered, namely, by a clear separation of political interests from all that is concerned with the representation, the administration, of economic interests. The impulse for the organization of the threefold order must, therefore, demand in the most emphatic manner, the separation of politics, and the groundwork of the law, from the administration of economic affairs, of the economic circuit. Within the economic circuit, as I explained yesterday, associations must be formed. Representatives of the different occupations should meet; producer and consumer should come together. The purely business operations and measures that take place should be based upon contracts entered into by the association. In the economic world everything should rest on contracts, everything should depend upon mutual service rendered. Corporations should carry on business with other corporations; expert knowledge and efficiency in particular branches should have the decisive voice. My opinion as a manufacturer, let us say, as to the importance of my particular branch of industry in political life will have no weight when the economic department is independent. I shall have to be productive in my own branch, to enter into contracts with the associations of other branches of industry and they will render me reciprocal services. If I am able to get a return of services for mine, I shall be in a position to carry on my work. An association of efficiency will be formed by means of contract. These are the facts of the case.

In the sphere of law and equity, affairs will be differently arranged. In that domain of life where one man meets another on equal terms, the only thing to be considered is the making of laws that shall regulate the rights of the public by the decisions of a majority. Of course, many will say, "What is really meant by public rights? It is neither more nor less than the spirit, expressed in the words and put into the form of laws, that animates the economic conditions." In many respects this is true, but the idea of the threefold social organism does not leave this out of consideration; in fact, it leaves no reality out of consideration. What results as just and equitable from the resolutions taken on the basis of the democratic state is introduced into the economic sphere by those who are occupied in industry, but it is not their work to initiate this spirit and to make laws. They receive the law and carry it into operation in the economic life.

Abstract thinkers raise objections to this threefold order. They say that in public life, when one man does business with another, gives a draft to another according to the law of exchange, the whole operation is carried on within the limits of the economic sphere. They ask, "Is that not a complete unity?" and say, "The idea of the threefold order tries to break up what is already a complete unity, as if there were not many spheres in life in which public opinion is not allowed to function lest it work destructively, many spheres in which forces from all sides meet and form a unity." Take the case of a young man. He has various hereditary qualities clinging to him. Then he has other qualities that he has acquired by education. His characteristics come to him from two sides, inheritance and education. Now suppose he does something at fifteen years of age; it cannot be said that such an action is isolated. His action is a unity composed of the result of heredity and education. There is unity in the action just because the forces come together from two sides. Out of the realities of life arises the idea of the threefold social organism. Real unity comes into an economic transaction only in proportion to the conceptions of justice it may contain, through the independent administration of economic measures from an economic standpoint, and through the making of laws by an independent democratic equity state. These two elements are then brought together into one whole. The two work as one. If, however, laws are allowed to arise out of the interests of economic life itself, the laws are turned into a caricature of justice. Law is then like a photograph or an impression of economic interests. There is no equity present.

Only when laws are allowed to arise naturally, and from the very beginning on their own independent democratic basis, can they be introduced into economic life.

One might think that this must be so obvious to all that explanation were quite unnecessary. But it is a peculiarity of this age that the most transparent truths are overshadowed by modern life, and that it is just those clearest facts that are most distorted. Many of the socialist views advanced at the present time make the continuation of the dependence of law on the economic life their basic principle. I alluded yesterday to the idea of founding a kind of hierarchy on political lines, according to which the economic life should be governed and administered. In this scheme it is thought that those who administer economic affairs will also, at the same time, develop the laws. This assertion proves an absolute lack of understanding of real life. It is not the economic system, in which efficiency above all things is necessary to promote production, that can bring forth suitable legal conditions; legal conditions must arise from their own source, side by side with the economic life. Laws can never be the outcome merely of thought. Side by side with the economic circuit exists a political element in which every single individual meets another on equal terms. The essential point is not that out of some vague primitive consciousness a businessman can evolve just laws, but that the soil itself should be first prepared, so that human beings might find themselves, through their feelings, in circumstances that they would transform into circumstances governed by law. The essential is to create a reality side by side with the economic life. Law will then no longer be a mere superstructure above the economic life; law will then take its place in a self-molding, independent existence. Then the fundamental error of the social question, the belief that the economic life need only be transformed in order to attain to new conceptions of law, will no longer be met by a theoretic answer. Then reality will be created in the threefold social organism by the preparation of an independent basis for political life, reality from which, through human intercourse and human relationship, the strong impetus towards a system of law and equity arises, capable of keeping the economic life within its proper limits.

Finally, a consideration of our age from the historical point of view reveals from another side in what manner all that I have said above can be proved. Look back to the period before the thirteenth and fourteenth centuries and think of the incentive given to the men of that period in their handicraft and in all other work. Modern socialist thinkers often emphasize the fact that the worker is separated from his means of production. That this is so to such a high degree at present is caused by modern economic conditions. Most of all he is separated from his products. What part has the factory worker in all that the manufacturer sells? What does he know about it? Often not even to what part of the world it goes. His work is a small part of a great complex, which perhaps he never sees as a whole. Think of the tremendous difference between present conditions and the old handicraft, when each man worked at his own product and took pleasure in his work! Anyone who has studied history can testify to this. Think of the personal relation between a workman and his handiwork, such as a door key, a lock, and so forth. In primitive regions of the country we can still find this feeling of a man towards his work. Where the customs are less simple, this is no longer possible. Forgive me if I mention a personal experience, it is characteristic of what I mean. I once entered a barber's shop in an out-of-the-way place and was truly happy to see the real pleasure taken by the barber's assistant in cutting a customer's hair nicely. His work was a real pleasure to him. There is, of course, always less and less of this personal tie between the worker and his work. Its absence is a condition of modern economic life, and it cannot be otherwise in the complicated circumstances arising out of the distribution of labor. If we had not the division of labor, however, neither should we have our modern life with all that is necessary to us. There would be no progress. The old connection between the workman and his work is no longer possible, but man needs a relationship to his work. It is necessary that he should feel joy in his work, that he should feel a certain devotion to it. The old devotion, the immediate companionship with the thing he has made, exists no longer; yet it must be replaced by something else. What can this be? It can only be replaced by enlarging men's horizon, by raising them to a level on which they can come together with their fellow men in one great circle, eventually with all their fellow men within the same social organism as themselves, in which they can develop an interest in man as man. It must come to pass that even the man who is working in the most remote corner at a single screw for some great machine need not put his whole self into the contemplation of the screw, but it must come about that he can carry into his workshop the feelings that he entertains for his fellow men, that when he leaves his workshop he finds the same feelings, that he has a living insight into his connection with human society, that he can work even without actual pleasure in his production because he feels he is a worthy member in the circle of his fellow men. Out of this impulse has sprung the modern demand for democracy and the new way of establishing public law on democratic lines. These things are related by their inner nature to the evolution of man. Only he who has the will to look deeply into the realities of human evolution in its progress in social life can really understand such things. The feeling must arise within us that the horizon of human beings must be enlarged, that men ought to be able to express their feelings with regard to their work in words somewhat like these, "It is true, I have no idea how my work in making this screw will affect my fellow men, but I do know that, through the living ties that bind me to them by a common law, I am a worthy member in the social order, and have equal rights with other men."

This is the principle that must lie at the root of modern democracy, and it must work in the feelings of one man towards another as the fundamental principle of the modern public legal code. Only by understanding the inner nature of the human being can we arrive at really modern conceptions of that common law that must now be developed everywhere. Details will be given on this head in the fifth lecture. In conclusion, I will now show how the sphere of justice passes over from the actual department of equity into that of cultural life.

We can see how laws arise on the basis of the democratic state by the refining of feelings among individuals with equal rights, while in the economic sphere of life, contracts are entered into between societies or between individuals. From the moment in which the individual finds himself in a position to seek justice under either civil or penal law, or in a private, or in any other manner, in that moment the decision passes from the purely legal to the cultural domain. Here is another point, similar to that discussed yesterday in dealing with taxation, that will present difficulties. It will take long for modern thinkers to accustom themselves to ideas that would demonstrate their self-evidence, if only their underlying conditions were examined.

Now when a case arises in which it has to be decided how an existing law can be applied to a particular person, we have to do with the exercise of an individual judgment. It must be determined whether the elected judge is really qualified by his mental and spiritual capacities to understand the person in question. Administration of punishment, civil justice, cannot rest on the general basis of law. It must be removed to another sphere, the special characteristics of which I will explain in my next lecture on the cultural life. Justice can only be administered when the judge is really able, by virtue of his own capacities, and out of the relationship between himself and the person whom he is trying, to give a verdict out of his own independent capacity of judging. One might perhaps think that this objective could be gained in various ways. In my book, *The Threefold Commonwealth*, I have pointed out one way in which it might be attained. In the threefold social organism there is (*a*) the independent economic organization described yesterday; (*b*) the democratic political foundation that I have sketched today and will develop more fully in my fifth lecture in regard to its interplay with the other members of the organism. There is also (*c*) the independent cultural life, which controls, above all things, teaching and education as I pointed out yesterday and which I will amplify in my next lecture. Those who control the cultural sphere will be called upon at the same time to appoint the judges, and every human being will be entitled and able to elect from time to time his own judge, should he find himself accused of an offense against civil or penal law. Thus the accused will be able, out of actual specific conditions, to appoint his own judge, and the judge, who will be no bureaucratic lawyer, but a man chosen out of the cultural sphere, through the circumstances in which he is placed in the social environment, will be able out of his environment to determine what judgment he must form of the man whom he is to try. It will be important that no judge shall be nominated for political reasons. The reasons for his nomination will be like those that determine the

72

nomination of the best teacher to a particular post. Becoming a judge will be something like becoming a teacher or an educator. Of course, in this way the judicial finding will differ from that laid down by the law arising from a democratic foundation. By the example of penal law already cited, we see how the personal disposition of the individual human being is outside the sphere of democracy and can only be judged in an individual way. The framing of laws is eminently a social matter. The moment we apply to a judge it is probably because we are concerned, either in a super-social or an anti-social matter, in a matter that has fallen out of the social life. All individual interests are of this nature. Such cases fall under the administrative branches of the cultural body. The decisions of justice grow beyond and above the limits of democracy.

So we see that what we have to do is to establish in reality conditions under which a genuine system of law can exist among men. Justice will then be no mere superstructure of the economic body, but equity will control economic life. We shall never succeed in doing what is necessary in this domain of life by a merely theoretical examination of the circumstances. It can be done in no other way than by a practical observation of life. This will give us the knowledge that a true system of justice with the necessary impetus can only arise on an independent foundation of law. This foundation has disappeared beneath the inundating flood of economic life. Politics and law have become dependent on the economic life, but they must regain their independence, just as cultural life must also be emancipated from the economic system. In order to see clearly in the social question, the great error must be overcome—the great error that we need only revolutionize economic conditions and then everything will follow automatically. That error has arisen in consequence of the all-powerful modern development of economic life alone. It is as if people were under the influence of an idea, as if they were under the suggestion that the economic life is the only power. As long as this suggestion holds sway they will never find the solution of the social problem. They will give themselves up to illusions, especially in proletarian circles. They will try to extract from the economic system what they call a just distribution of property. But this will only be effected when there are men in the social organism possessing the ability to promote institutions through which the economic needs can be satisfied. That can only happen when it is understood that the revolutionizing of the economic system is not the only thing necessary to satisfy the requirements of social life. People must first answer the question: Must not something else be there alongside the economic body in order that the economic life may be built up continuously in a social manner by men who have grown social in political and in cultural life? This is the truth that we must oppose to error and dogma, and those who look to the economic life for the means of restoring health to the social organism must look instead to the spirit and to justice. There must be no vague dreams of justice growing out of the economic system; we must cultivate right thought in accordance with realities, and we must do so because justice and the consciousness of justice have retreated in later times before the advancing economic flood. For a social construction of society, we need the creation of a genuine political organism with the social impetus necessary for it.

IV

CULTURAL QUESTIONS. SPIRITUAL SCIENCE (ART, SCIENCE, RELIGION). THE NATURE OF EDUCATION. SOCIAL ART.

When we review the history of the last few years and ask ourselves how the social problems and needs occupying the public mind for more than half a century have been dealt with, we can find only one answer. Although in the greater part of the civilized world, opportunity to carry out in practice their ideas of reconstructing social life was given to people who, after their own fashion, had devoted themselves for decades to the study of social problems, yet it must be regarded as characteristic of the age that all the theories and views that are the result of half a century of social work from every quarter have shown themselves powerless to reconstruct the present social conditions.

Of late years much has been destroyed and, in the eyes of all observant persons, little, or probably nothing, built up. Does not the question force itself here upon the human soul: What is the cause of this impotence of so-called advanced views, in the face of some positive task? Shortly before the great catastrophe of the World

War, in the spring of 1914, I ventured to answer this question in a short series of lectures I delivered in Vienna before a small audience. A larger number of hearers would probably have treated what was said with ridicule. In regard to all the assumptions of the so-called experts in practical affairs as to the immediate future, I ventured to say that an exact observer of the inner life of humanity could see in the social conditions prevailing all over the civilized world something like an abscess, like a social disease, a kind of cancerous growth, that must inevitably soon break out in a terrible manner over this world. Those practical statesmen, who were then talking of the "improvement in political relations" and the like, looked upon this as the pessimism of an idealist. But that was the utterance of a conviction gained by a study of human evolution from the point of view of spiritual science, which I will describe to you this evening. To this kind of research the building known as the Dornach Building, the Goetheanum, is dedicated. Situated in the corner of the northwest of Switzerland, this building is the outer representation of the movement whose object is the study of the spiritual science of which I speak. You will hear and read all kinds of assertions about the aims and object of this building and the meaning of the movement it is intended to represent. It may be said in most cases that the gossip about these things is the very opposite of the truth. Mysterious nonsense, false and senseless mysticism, many varieties of obscure nonsense are attached to the work attempted by this movement in the building at Dornach representing it. It cannot be expected that anything but misunderstandings without number should still exist regarding this movement of spiritual life. In reality, the meaning of the movement is to be found in its striving with set purpose to bring about a renewal of our whole civilization, as it is expressed in art, religion, science, education and other human activities; in fact, it may truly be said that a renewal is sorely needed from the foundations of social life upwards. This stream of spiritual life leads us to the conviction, already indicated by me in these lectures, that it is no longer of any use to devise new schemes for world-improvement; from its very nature, human evolution demands a transformation of thoughts and ideas of the most intimate life of feeling of humanity itself. Such a transformation is the aim of spiritual science, as it is represented in this movement. Spiritual science stimulates the belief that the views of society, of which we have just spoken, proceed from the old habits of thought that have not kept pace with the evolution of humanity and are no longer suited to its present life. These views have been clearly proved useless in aiding the reconstruction of social life.

What we need is understanding. What is really the meaning of all the subconscious yearnings, of the demands, which have not yet penetrated into the conscious thought of our present humanity? What do they mean, above all things, with regard to art, with regard to science, religion, and education? Let us look at the new directions followed by art, especially of late! I know well that in giving the following little sketch of the development of art, I must inevitably give offense to many; indeed, what I am going to say will be taken by many as a proof of the most complete lack of understanding of the later schools of art.

If we except a few isolated, commendable efforts of recent years, the chief characteristic in the development of modern art is that it has lost the inner impulse that should drive it to place before the world what is felt by humanity as a pressing need. The opinion has grown ever more common that, in contemplating a work of art, we must ask, "How much of the spirit and significance of outer reality does it express? How far is external nature or human life reflected in

77

art?" One need only ask what meaning such a criterion has with respect to a "Raphael," or a "Leonardo," or to any other real work of art. Do we not see in such great works of art that the resemblance to the outer reality surrounding us is by no means the measure of their greatness? Do we not see the measure of their greatness in the creation of something from within that is far removed from the immediate outer reality? What worlds are those that unroll before us as we gaze at the now almost effaced painting at Milan, Leonardo's *Last Supper,* or when we stand before a Raphael? Is it not a matter of secondary importance that those painters have succeeded more or less well in depicting the laws of nature in their work? Is it not their chief aim to tell us something of a world that we do not see when we only use our eyes, when we perceive only with our outer senses? Do we not find more and more that the only criterion now applied in judging a work of art, or in judging anything artistic, is whether the thing is really true, and "true" here is to be understood in the ordinary naturalistic sense of the word. Let us ask ourselves—strange as the question may appear to the holders of certain artistic views—what does an art confer on life, actually on social life, what is an art that aspires to nothing higher than the reproduction of a part of external reality?

At the time in which modern capitalism and modern technical science became a power, landscape painting began to be developed in the world of art. I know, of course, that landscape painting is justified, fully justified from an artistic point of view. But it is also true, that no artistically perfect landscape painting, however perfect, equals in any sense the scene lying before me, as I stand on a mountain side and contemplate nature's own landscape. Precisely the rise of landscape painting shows to what an extent art has taken refuge in the mere imitation of nature, which it can never equal. Art turned to landscape painting because it had lost touch with the spiritual world; it could no longer create out of the spiritual and supersensible world. What will be the future of art, if it is inspired only by the recent impulses toward naturalistic art? Art such as this can never grow out of life, as a flower grows from its roots; it will be a luxury outside life, an object of desire for those only for whom life has no cares. Is it not comprehensible that people who are absorbed in the pressing cares of life from morning till evening, who are shut off from all culture, the object of which is the understanding of art, should feel themselves separated as by an abyss from art? Though one hardly dares to put the sentiment into words nowadays, because to many it would stamp the speaker as a philistine, it is distinctly evident in social life that great numbers of people look on art as something remote, and unconsciously feel it to be a luxury of life, something that does not belong to every human life, and to every existence worthy of a human being, although, in truth, it brings completion to every human life worthy of the name.

Naturalistic art will always be in one sense a luxury for those whose lives are free from care, and who are able to educate themselves in that art. I felt this when I was teaching for some years in a working men's college, where I had the opportunity of addressing the workers themselves directly in order to help them understand the socialist theories that were being instilled into their minds, to their ruin, by those who called themselves "leaders of the people." I learned to understand—forgive the personal remark—what it means to bring scientific knowledge from a purely human standpoint within reach of those unspoiled minds. From a longing to know something also about modern art a request was made by my students that I take them through the museums and picture galleries on Sundays. Though it was possible, of course, to explain a great deal to them, since they had themselves the desire to be educated, I knew quite well that what I said did not at all make the same impression on these minds as did the things that I had told them from the standpoint of universal humanity. I felt that it would be a cultural untruth to tell them about the luxury art of the later naturalistic school, so far removed from actual life. This on the one hand.

On the other hand, do we not see how art has lost its connection with life? Here, too, praiseworthy endeavors have come to light in the last few decades, but these have been by no means decided enough, though much has been done in the direction of industrial art. We see how inartistic our everyday surroundings have become. Art has made an illusory progress. All the buildings around us with which we come in contact in our daily routine are as devoid of artistic beauty as possible. Practical life cannot be raised to artistic form because art has separated itself from life. Art that merely imitates nature cannot design tables and chairs and other articles of utility in such a manner that when we see them, we at once have the feeling of something artistic. These objects must transcend nature as human life transcends itself. If art merely imitates, it fails in the shaping of practical life, and practical life thereby becomes prosaic, uninteresting and dry because we are unable to give it an artistic form and to surround ourselves with beautiful objects in our everyday lives.

This might be further amplified. I shall only indicate the decided direction the evolution of our art has nevertheless taken. We have moved in like manner in other domains of modern civilization. Have we not seen that science has gradually ceased to proclaim to us the foundation that lies at the base of all sensory life? Little wonder that art has not found the way out of the world of sense since science itself has lost that way. By degrees science has come to the point of merely registering the outer facts of the senses, or at most to comprise them in natural laws. Intellectualism of the most pronounced type has overspread all modern scientific activity to an ever increasing degree, and a terrible fear prevails among scientists lest they should be unable to exclude everything but intellectualism in their research, lest something like imaginative or artistic intuitions should perchance find their way into science. It is easy to see by what is said and written on this subject by scientists themselves how great is the terror they experience at the thought that any other means than the dry, sober intellect and the investigation by sense perception should find entrance into scientific research. In every activity that does not keep strictly to intellectual thought men do not get far enough away from outer reality to judge it correctly. Thus the modern researcher, the modern scientist, strives to carry on his work by intellectualism only because he believes he can by this means get away far enough from the reality to judge it, as he says, quite objectively. Here the question might perhaps be asked, "Is it not possible through intellectualism to get so far away from reality that we can no longer experience it?" It is this intellectualism, above all, that has made it impossible for us to conquer reality by science, as I have already indicated in these lectures and into which I will enter more fully today.

Turning to the religious life, with what mistrust and disapproval is every attempt to penetrate into the spiritual world by means of spiritual science received by the religious communities! On what grounds? People are quite ignorant of the reason of their disapproval. From official quarters we learn of a science that is determined to keep to the mere world of the senses, and we hear that in these official quarters the claim is apparently allowed that it is only in this way that strict and true scientific knowledge can be attained.

But the student of historical evolution does not view the matter in this light. To him it appears that for the last few centuries the religious bodies have more and more laid claim to be the only authority in matters relating to the spirit and soul, and have recognized as valid only those opinions that they themselves permit the people to hold. Under the influence of this claim to the monopoly of knowledge by the Church, the sciences have neglected the study of everything except the outer sense perceptions, or at most they have attempted to penetrate into the higher regions with a few abstract conceptions. They believe they are doing this purely in the interests of exact science, and do not dream that they are influenced by the Church's pretension to the monopoly of knowledge, the knowledge of the spirit and the soul as contained in their religious creeds. What has been forbidden to the sciences for centuries, the sciences themselves now declare to be an absolute condition for the exactness of their research, for the objective truth of their work. Thus it has happened that the religious communities, having failed to develop their insight into the world of soul and spirit, and having preserved the old traditions, now see in the new methods of spiritual research, in the new paths of approach to the soul and spirit, an enemy to all religion, whereas they ought to recognize in these new methods the very best friends of religion.

We shall now speak of these three regions of culture, art, science, and religion, for it is the mission of anthroposophy or spiritual science to build up a new structure in these three regions of culture. To explain what I mean, I must indicate in a few words the vital point of spiritual science. Its premises are different from those of science as it is commonly known today. It fully recognizes the methods of modern science, fully recognizes also the triumphs of modern science. But because spiritual science believes it understands the methods of research of modern science better than the scientists themselves, it feels compelled to take other ways for the attainment of knowledge regarding spirit and soul than those that are still regarded by large numbers of people as the only right ones. In consequence of the enormous prejudice entertained against all research into the higher worlds, great errors and misunderstandings have been spread abroad regarding the aims of the Dornach movement. That there is truly no false mysticism, nothing in any way obscure in this movement, is plainly evident in my endeavors in the beginning of the 'nineties, which formed the starting-point for the spiritual-scientific movement to which I allude, and of which the building at Dornach is the representative. At that time I collected the material that seemed to me then most necessary for the social enlightenment of today in my *Philosophy of Freedom*. Whoever reads that book will hardly accuse the spiritual science of which I speak of false mysticism, but he may see what a difference there is between the idea of human freedom contained in my book and the idea of freedom as an impulse prevalent in our modern civilization.

As an example of the latter, I might give Woodrow Wilson's idea of freedom—an extraordinary one, but characteristic of the culture, the civilization of our age. He is honest in his demand for freedom for the political life of the present day. But what does he mean by freedom? We arrive at an understanding of his meaning when we read words like the following, "A ship moves freely," he says, "when it is adapted to all the forces that act upon it from the wind, from the waves, and so on. When its construction is exactly adapted to its environment, no hindrance to its progress can arise through the forces of wind or wave. Man must also be able to move freely through life, by adapting himself to the forces with which he comes in contact in life, so that no hindrance may ever come to him from any direction." He also compares the life of a free human being with a part of a machine, saying, "We say of a part built into a machine, that it can move freely when it has no connection with anything anywhere, and when the rest of the machine is so constructed that this part runs freely within it."

I have just one thing to say to this. We can only speak of freedom with regard to the human being when we see in it the very opposite of such an adaptation to the environment. We can only speak of human freedom when we compare it, not with the freedom of a ship on the sea, perfectly adapted to the forces of wind and weather, but when we compare it with the freedom of a ship that can stop and turn against wind and weather, and can do so without regarding the forces to which it is adapted. That is to say, at the bottom of such an idea of freedom as this lies the whole mechanical conception of the world, yet today it is considered to be the only possible one. This world conception is the result of the mere intellectualism of modern times. In my *Philosophy of Freedom* I have felt compelled to take a stand against views of this kind. I know very well—forgive another personal remark—that this book has fragments of the European philosophical conception of the world, out of which it is born, still clinging to it, as a chicken sometimes retains fragments of the shell from which it has emerged, for the book has, of course, grown out of European philosophical world conceptions. It was necessary to show in that book the erroneous thought in those world conceptions. For this reason the book may appear to some to be pedantic, though this was by no means my intention. The contents are intended to work as an impulse in the immediate practice of life, so that, through the ideas developed in that book, the impulse thus generated in the human will may flow directly into human life.

For this reason, however, I was obliged to state the problem of human freedom quite differently from the usual manner of doing so. Wherever we turn throughout the centuries of human evolution, the question regarding the freedom of human will and of the human being has been: Is man free, or is he not free? I was under the necessity of showing that the question in this form was wrongly framed and must be put from a different standpoint. If we take what modern science and modern human consciousness look upon as the *real self,* but which ought to be regarded as the *natural self,* then, certainly, that being can never be free. That self must act of inner necessity. Were man only what he is held to be by modern science, then his idea of freedom would be the same as that of Woodrow Wilson's. This would be no real freedom. It would be only what might be called with every single action the inevitable result of natural causes. But modern human consciousness is not much aware of the other self within the human being where the problem regarding freedom really begins. Modern human consciousness is only aware of the *natural self* in man; it regards him as a being subject to natural causality. Those who penetrate more deeply into the human being must reflect that man can become something more in the course of his life than only with what nature has endowed him. We first discover what the human being really is when we recognize that one part of him is that with which he is born, and all that he has inherited; the other part is what he does not owe to his bodily nature, but that he can make of himself by awakening the *real self* slumbering within him. Because these things are true I have not asked: Is man free or not free? I have stated the question in the following way. Can man become a free being through inner development, or can he not? The answer is: He can become free if he develops within himself what otherwise slumbers, but can be awakened;

he can only then become free. Man's freedom is not a gift of nature. Freedom belongs to the part of man that he can, and must, awaken within himself. If the ideas contained in my *Philosophy of Freedom* are to be further developed and applied to external social life, so that these truths may become clear to a larger circle of people, it will be necessary to build a superstructure of the truths of spiritual science on the foundation of that philosophy. It had to be shown that by taking his evolution into his own hands, man is really able to awaken a slumbering being within him. I endeavored to do this in my book, *Knowledge of the Higher Worlds,* and in the other books that I have contributed to the literature of spiritual science. In these books I tried to show that the human being can indeed take his own evolution in hand and that only by so doing and thus making of it something different from that to which he is born, can he rise to a real knowledge of soul and spirit. It is true that this view is considered by a large part of humanity at the present day to be a most unattractive one. For what does it presuppose? It presupposes that we attain to something like intellectual humility, but few desire this today. I will explain what I mean by this quality of intellectual humility to which we must attain.

Suppose we give a volume of Goethe's lyric poems to a child of five. The child will certainly not treat the book as it deserves; he will tear it to pieces, or spoil it in some other way. In any case he does not know how to value such a book. But suppose the child to have grown ten or twelve years older, that he has been taught and trained; then he will treat Goethe's lyric poems in a different manner. Yet there is no great difference externally between a child of five and one of twelve or fourteen with a book of Goethe's poems before him. The difference lies within the child. He has developed so that he knows what to do with such a volume. As the child feels towards the volume of Goethe's lyrics, so must the man feel towards nature, the cosmos, the whole universe, when he begins to think seriously of soul and spirit. He must acknowledge to himself that, in order to read and understand what is written in the book of nature and the universe, he must do his utmost to develop his inner self, just as the five year old child must be taught in order to understand Goethe's lyric poems. We must acknowledge with intellectual humility our impotence to penetrate the universe with understanding by means of the natural gifts with which we are born, and we must then admit that there may be ways of self-development and of unfolding the inner powers of our being to see in what lies spread out before the senses the living spirit and the living soul. My writings to which I have referred show that it is possible to put this into practice. This must be said, because intellectualism, the fruit of evolution of the last few centuries, is no longer able to solve the riddles of life. Into one region of life, that of inanimate nature, it is able to penetrate, but it is compelled to halt before human reality, more especially social reality.

The quality I have called intellectual humility must be the groundwork of every true modern conception of the impulse towards freedom. It must also be the groundwork of all real insight into the transformation necessary in art, religion, and science. Here intellectuality has only too plainly shown that it can attain no real knowledge that truly perceives and attains to the things of the soul and spirit. As I have already pointed out, it has confined itself to the outer world of the senses and to the combining and systematizing of perceptions. Hence it has been unable to prevail against the pretensions of the religious bodies, which have also not attained to a new knowledge of matters pertaining to the soul and spirit, but have on this account carried into modern times an antiquated view, unsuited to the age. One thing must be conquered, that is the fear I have already described, the fear that we might become too much involved in the objects of the senses, in our endeavors to gain a spiritual knowledge of them. It is so easy to call oneself a follower of intellectualism, because, when we occupy ourselves merely with abstract ideas, even of modern science, we are so far removed from the reality that we only view it in perspective, and there is no danger of our being in any way influenced by the reality. But with the knowledge that is meant here, which we gain for ourselves when we take our own evolution in hand, with such knowledge we must descend into the realities of life; we must plunge into the profoundest depths of our own nature, deeper than those reached by mere self-training in intellectualism. Within the bounds of intellectualism, we only reach the upper strata of our own life. If with the help of the knowledge here spoken of, we descend into the depths of our own inner nature, we find there not only thoughts and feelings, a mere reflection of the outer world. We find there happenings, facts of our inner being, from which the merely intellectual thinker would recoil in horror, but they are of the same kind as those within nature itself, of the same kind as those that happen in the world. Then, within our own nature, we learn to know the nature of the world. We cannot learn to know that life of the world if we go no further than mere abstract conceptions or the laws of nature. We must penetrate so far that our own inmost being becomes one with reality. We must not fear to approach reality; our inner development must carry us so far that we can stand firm in the presence of reality, without being consumed, or scorched, or suffocated. When we stand in the presence of reality, no longer held at a distance by the intellect, we are able to grasp the truth of things. Thus, we find described in my book, *Knowledge of the Higher Worlds*, the inner development of the human being to the stage of spiritual knowledge at which he becomes one with reality, but in such wise that, being merged in reality, he can imbibe from it knowledge that is not a distant perception by means of the intellect, but is instead saturated with reality itself and for this reason can merge with it.

You will find that one characteristic feature of the spiritual science that occupies us here is that it can plunge into reality, that it does not merely speak of an abstract spirit, but of the real, tangible spirit, living in our environment surrounding us just as the things of the sensory world surround us. Abstract observations are the fruit of modern intellectualism. Take up any new work, with the exception of pure natural science or pure philosophy, and you will find the conception of life it contains, often a would-be philosophical view, is far removed from actual life or from a real knowledge of things. Read what is said about the will in one of the newer books on psychology, and you will find that there is no profound meaning underlying the words. The ideas of those who devote themselves to such studies have not the power actually to penetrate to the core, even of nature itself. To them matter is a thing outside because they cannot penetrate it in spirit. I should like to elucidate this by an example.

In one of my last books, *Riddles of the Soul*,* I have shown how an opinion of long standing, prevailing in natural science, must be overcome by modern spiritual science. I know how paradoxical my words must sound to many. But it is just those truths that are able to satisfy the demands—already making themselves heard and becoming more and more insistent as time goes on—for a new kind of thought that will often appear paradoxical, when compared with all

---

* Excerpts from this book have been published with the title, *The Case for Anthroposophy.*

that is still looked upon as authoritative. Every modern scientist who has occupied himself with the subject maintains that there are two kinds of nerves in human and animal life (we are now only concerned with human life); one set, leading from the sense organs to the central organ, is the sensory nerves, which are stimulated by sense perceptions, the stimulus communicating itself to the nerve center. The second kind of nerves, the so-called motor nerves, pass from the center out to the limbs. These motor nerves enable us to use our limbs. They are said to be the nerves of volition, while the others are called the sensory nerves.

Now I have shown in my book, *Riddles of the Soul*, though only in outline, that there is no fundamental difference between the sensory and the so-called motor nerves or nerves of volition, and that the latter are not subject to the will. The instances brought forward to support the statement that these nerves are obedient to the will as is shown by the terrible disease of *locomotor ataxia* really prove the exact opposite, which can easily be shown. They, indeed, prove the truth of my contention. These so-called voluntary nerves are also sensory nerves. While the other sensory nerves pass from the sense organs to the central organ, so that the outer sense perceptions may be transmitted to it, the voluntary nerves, as they are called, which do not differ from the other set, perceive what is movement within ourselves. They are endowed with the perception of movement. There are no voluntary nerves. The will is of a purely spiritual nature, purely spirit and soul, and functions directly as spirit and soul. We use the so-called voluntary nerves, because they are the sensory nerves for the limb that is going to move and must be perceived if the will is to move it. For what reason do I give this example? Because countless treatises on the will exist at the present day, or may be read and heard, in which the will is dealt with, but the ideas developed have not the impelling power to advance to real knowledge, to press forward to the sight of will in its working. Such knowledge remains abstract and foreign to life. While such ideas are current, modern science will continue to tell us of motor nerves, of nerves of volition. Spiritual science evolves ideas regarding the will that show us at the same time the nature of the physical human nervous system. Spiritual science will penetrate the phenomena and facts of nature. Instead of remaining in regions foreign to life, it will find its way into reality. It will have the courage to permeate material things with the spirit, not to leave them outside as things apart. For spiritual science everything is spiritual. Spiritual science will be able to pierce the surface and penetrate into the social order, and will work for a reality in social life, which baffles our abstract, intellectual natural science. Thus, spiritual science will again proclaim a spiritual knowledge, a new way of penetrating into the psychic and the spiritual in the universe. It will proclaim boldly that those spiritual worlds, represented in pictures envisioned by artists such as Raphael, Michelangelo, and Leonardo da Vinci, can no longer suffice for us. In accordance with the progress of human evolution, we must find a new way into the spiritual world. If we learn to understand the spiritual world anew, if we penetrate into that world, not in the nebulous manner of pantheism by a continual repetition of the word "spirit," a universal, abstract, vague spirit which "must be there"; if we pierce through to the real phenomena of the spiritual world not by spiritualism, but by the development of the human forces of spirit and soul in the manner described above, then again we shall know of a spiritual world in the only way adapted to the present development of humanity. Then the mysteries of the spiritual world will reveal themselves to us, and then something will happen of which Goethe spoke. Although he

91

was only a beginner in the things that modern spiritual science goes on developing in accordance with his own spirit, but of which he had a premonition, Goethe beautifully expressed what will happen in the words, "He to whom nature begins to reveal its open secrets, experiences a profound longing for its worthiest exponent—art." Once more will the artist receive a revelation from the spiritual world. He will then no longer be led astray in the belief that his portrayal of spiritual things in a material picture is an abstract, symbolic, lifeless allegory. He will know the living spirit and will be able to express that living spirit through material means. No longer will the perfect imitation of nature be considered the best part of a work of art, but the manifestation of what the spirit has revealed to the artist. Once more an art will arise filled with spirit, an art in no way symbolical, in no way allegorical, which also does not betray its luxurious character by attempting to rival nature, to the perfection of which it can never attain. It demonstrates its necessity, its justification, in human life by proclaiming the existence of something of which the ordinary, direct beholding of nature, naturalism, can give us no information. Even if the artist's attempt to give expression to something spiritual be but a clumsy effort, he is giving form to something that has a significance apart from nature because it transcends nature. He makes no bungling attempts at what nature can do better than he. A way opens here to that art in which a beginning has been made in the external structure and the external decoration of the Goetheanum at Dornach.

The attempt has been made there to create a University of Spiritual Science for the work to be carried on within it. In all the paintings on the ceilings, the wood carvings, etc., an attempt has been made to give form to all that spiritual science reveals in that building. Hence the building itself is a natural development. No old architectural style could be followed here, because the spirit will be spoken of in a new way within it. Let us look at nature and consider the shell of a nut; the kernel within determines the form of it; in nature every sheath is formed in accordance with the requirements of the inner core. So the whole of the building at Dornach is formed in consonance with what as music will one day resound within it; with those mystery dramas that will one day be presented there; with those revelations of spiritual science that will one day be uttered within its walls. Everything described there will echo in the wood carvings, in the pillars and in the capitals. An art as yet only in its beginnings, which is really born of a new spirit, altogether born of the spirit, is there represented. The artists who are working there are themselves their own severest critics. In such an undertaking one is, of course, exposed to misunderstandings; this is only natural. Objections are raised against the Dornach Building by visitors, who say, "These anthroposophists have filled their building with symbols and allegories." Other visitors who increase in number from day to day, understand what they see there.

Now the characteristic of the building is that it does not contain a single symbol or allegory; in the work attempted there the spirit has flowed into the immediate artistic form. What is expressed there has nothing of symbolism, nothing of allegory, but everything is something in its own form. Up to the present we have only been able to build a covering for a spiritual center of work; external social conditions do not yet permit us to erect a railway station or even a bank building. For reasons that may perhaps be easily comprehensible to you we have not yet been able to find the style of a modern bank or of a modern department store, but they must also be found. Above all things, the way must be found along these lines to an artistic shaping of actual practical life.

93

Just think of the social importance of art, even for our daily bread, for the preparation of bread depends on the manner in which people think and feel.

It is a matter of great and social significance to men, that everything by which they are immediately surrounded in life should take on an artistic form. Every spoon, every glass, should have a form well adapted to its use, instead of a form chosen at random to serve the purpose. One should see at a glance, from its form, what service a thing performs in life, and at the same time recognize its beauty. Then for the first time large numbers of people will feel spiritual life to be a vital necessity, when spiritual life and practical life are brought into direct connection with each other. As spiritual science is able to throw light on the nature of matter, as I have shown in the example of the sensory and motor nerves, so will art, born of spiritual science, attain to the power of giving direct form to every chair, every table, to every man-created object.

Since it is plainly evident that the gravest prejudices and misunderstandings come from the churches, we may ask what the position is that is finally reached by the religious creeds. If they have any justification at all, they must have a connection by their very nature with the spiritual world. But they have preserved and carried into our period of time old traditions of these worlds, grown out of different conditions of the human soul. Spiritual science strives to advance to the spiritual world, in accordance with the new mode of thought, with the new life of the soul. Should this be condemned by the religious sentiment of humanity, if it understands itself aright? Is such a thing possible? Never! What is the real aim of religious sentiment and of all religious work? Certainly not the proclamation of theories and dogmas pertaining to the higher worlds. The aim of all religious work should be to give all men an opportunity to look up with reverence to higher worlds. The work of religion is to inculcate reverence for the supersensible. Human nature needs this reverence. It needs to look up in reverence to the sublime in the spiritual worlds. If human nature is denied the present mode of entrance, then, of course, the old way must still be kept open, but since this way is no longer suited to the thoughts of our day, it must be enforced; its recognition must be imposed by authority. Hence the external character of religious teaching as applied to modern human nature. An antiquated outlook on the higher worlds is imposed by the religious teachers.

Let us suppose that there are communities in which an understanding exists of the true nature of religion consisting in reverence for spiritual things. Must it not be to the highest interest of such communities that their members should develop a living knowledge of the unseen world? Will not those whose souls contain a vision of the supersensible, whose knowledge gives them a familiarity with those worlds be the most likely to reverence them? Since the middle of the fifteenth century human evolution has taken the line of development of the individuality, of the personality. To expect of anyone today that he should attain a vision or an understanding of the higher worlds on authority, or in any other way than by the force of his own individuality or personality, is to expect of him something that is against his nature. If he is allowed freedom of thought with respect to his knowledge of the supersensible he will unite with his fellow men in order that reverence for the spiritual world, which everyone recognizes in his own personal way, may be encouraged in the community. When men have attained freedom of thought to approach knowledge of the spiritual world through their own individuality, then the common service of the higher worlds, true religion, will flourish.

This will show itself especially in the conception of the Christ Himself. This conception was different in earlier centuries from that even of many theologians of the later centuries, especially of the nineteenth. How greatly has humanity fallen away from the perception of the true supersensible nature of the Christ, who lived in the man Jesus! How far is it removed from the understanding of that union of a supersensible being with a human body, through the Mystery of Golgotha, in order that the earth in its development might have a deeper meaning! That union of the supersensible with the things of the senses, which was consummated in the Mystery of Golgotha, how little has it been understood even by theologians of a certain type in recent times! The man of Nazareth has been designated "the simple man of Nazareth," the conception of religion has become more and more materialistic. Since no one was able to find a way into the higher worlds suited to modern humanity, the supersensible path to the Christ Being was lost. Many who now believe that they are in communion with the Christ, only *believe* this. They do not dream how little their thought of Christ and their words concerning Him correspond to the experiences of those who draw near to the great mystery of humanity with a spiritual knowledge that is suited to our time.

It must be said that spiritual science makes absolutely no pretension of founding a new religion. It is a science, a source of knowledge, but we ought to recognize in it the means for a rejuvenescence of the religious life of humanity. As it can rejuvenate science and art, so can it also renew religious life, the great importance of which must be apparent to anyone who can appreciate the extreme gravity of the social future.

Much, very much has been said recently on the subject of education, yet it must be acknowledged that a large part of the discussion does not touch the chief problem. I endeavored to deal with this problem in a series of educational lectures that I was asked to deliver to the teachers who are to form the staff of the Waldorf School in Stuttgart, which was founded last September [1919], in conformity with ideas underlying the threefold social order.

At the foundation of the school I not only endeavored to give shape to externals, corresponding to the requirements and the impulse of the threefold order. I also strove to present pedagogy and didactics to the teaching staff of this new kind of school in such a light that the human being would be educated to face life and be able to bring about a social future in accordance with certain unconquerable instincts in human nature. It is evident that the old-fashioned system of normal training, with its stereotyped rules and methods of teaching, must be superseded. It is true nowadays that many people agree that the individuality of the pupil ought to be taken into account in teaching. All sorts of rules are produced for the proper consideration of the child's individuality, but the pedagogy of the future will not be a normal science. It will be a true art, the art of developing the human being. It will rest upon a knowledge of the whole man. The teacher of the future will know that in the human being before him, who carries on development from birth through all the years of life, a spirit and soul element is working through the organs out to the surface. From the first year of school, he will see how every year new forces evolve from the depths of the child's nature. No abstract normal training can confirm this sight but only a living perception of human nature itself. Much has been said of late on the subject of instruction through observation and, within certain limits, this kind of tuition is justified. But there are things that cannot be communicated through external observation, yet they must be communicated to

97

the growing child. They can only be so communicated when the teacher, the educator, is animated by a true understanding of the growing human being, when he is able to see the inner growth of the child as it changes with every succeeding year; when he knows what the inner nature of the human being requires in the seventh, ninth, and twelfth years of his life. For only when education is carried on in accordance with nature can the child grow strong for the battle of life. One comes in contact with many shattered lives today, many who do not know what to make of life, to whom it has nothing to offer. There are many more people who suffer from such disrupted lives than is commonly known. What is the reason? It is because the teacher is unable to take note of important laws of the evolving human being. I will give only one instance of what I mean. How often do we hear well-meaning teachers say emphatically that one should develop in the child a clear understanding of what is being offered him as mental food. The result of this method in practice is banality, triviality! The teacher descends artificially to the understanding of the child, and that manner of teaching has already become instinctive. If it is persisted in, and the child is trained in this false clarity of understanding, what is overlooked? A teacher of this kind does not know what it means to a man, say thirty-five years of age, who looks back to his childhood and remembers, "My teacher told me such and such a thing when I was nine or ten years old; I believed it because I looked up with reverence to the authority of my teacher, and because there was a living force in his personality through which I was impressed by his words. Now, looking back, I find that his words have lived on in me; now I can understand them." A marvelous light is shed on life by such an event, when through inner development we can look back in our thirty-fifth year at the lessons we have learned out of love for our teacher that we could not understand at the time. That light, which is a force in life, is lost when the teacher descends to the banality of the object-lesson that is praised as an ideal method. The teacher must know what forces should be developed in the child, in order that the forces already in his nature may remain with him throughout his life. Then the child need not merely recall to memory what he learned between his seventh and fifteenth years; what he then learned is renewed again and again, and wears a new aspect in each successive stage of life. What the child learned is renewed at every later epoch of life.

The foregoing is an effort to place before you an idea of the fundamental character of a system of pedagogy that, if followed, may truly grow into an art. By its practice the human being may take his place in life and find himself equal to all the demands of the social future. However much people may vaunt their social ideals, there are few who are at all capable of surveying life as a whole, but in the carrying out of social ideals, a wide outlook on life is indispensable. People speak, for instance, of transferring the means of production to the ownership of the community and believe that by withdrawing them from the administration of the individual human being, much would be accomplished. I have already spoken on this point, and will go into the subject again more thoroughly in the following lectures. But assuming for a moment that it is possible to transfer the means of production to the ownership of the community at once, do you suppose that the community of the next generation would still own them? No! For even if the means of production were transmitted to the next generation, it would be done without taking into account the fact that this next generation would develop new and fruitful forces that would transform the whole system of production, thus rendering the old means useless. If we have any idea of molding social life, we must take part in life in its fullness, in all its phases. From a conception of man as a being composed of body, soul and spirit, and from a real understanding of body, soul and spirit, a new art of education will arise, an art that may truly be regarded as a necessity in social life.

Arising from this way of thinking, something has developed within the spiritual movement centered at Dornach that has to a great extent met with misunderstanding. There are a number of persons who have learned in the course of years to think not unfavorably of our spiritual-scientific movement. When we recently began, in Zürich and elsewhere, to give representations of the art known as eurythmy, an art springing naturally out of spiritual science itself, but, as we are fully aware, as yet only in its infancy, people began to exclaim that after all, spiritual science cannot be worth much, for to introduce such antics as an accompaniment to spiritual science only shows that the latter is completely crazy. In such a matter as this, people do not consider how paradoxical anything must appear that works toward reconstituting the world on the basis of spiritual science. This art of eurythmy is a social art in the best sense; its aim is, above all things, to communicate to us the mysteries of human nature. It uses the capacities for movement latent in the human being, bringing to expression these movements in a manner to be explained at the next representation of the eurythmic art. I will only mention here that eurythmy is a true art; it reveals the deepest secrets of human art itself by bringing to evidence a true speech, a visible speech expressed by the whole human being. But beside the mere movements of the body, founded on physiological science and a study of the structure of the human form, eurythmy presents to us at the same time a capacity of movement through which man, ensouled and inspired, yields himself up to movement. The purely

100

physiological, gymnastic exercises of our materialistic age may also be taught to children, and they are now taught in the Waldorf School of which I have spoken. Ensouled movement, however, actually employs the whole being, while gymnastics on physiological, merely material lines employs only a part of the whole nature of the human being, and therefore, unless supplemented by eurythmy, allows much to degenerate in the growing human being. Out of the depths of human nature spiritual life in a new form must enter into the most important branches of life.

It will be my task in the next few days to show how external life may really be given a new form in the present and for the future, when the impulse for the change comes from such a new spirit. Many people of all sorts, noteworthy people, feel today the necessity of understanding spiritually the modern pressing demands of social life. It is painful to see the number of people who are still asleep as regards these demands, and the many others who approach them in a confused way as agitators. We find faint indications of a feeling that none of the mere superficial programs can be of any use without a change of thought, of ideas, a new mode of learning from the spirit. But in many cases how superficial is the expression of that longing for a new spirit! We may say that the yearning for a new spirit is dimly and imperceptibly felt here and there in remarkable men, who most certainly have no idea of what the Dornach Building represents in the outer world. But the expression of a longing for this new spirit can be heard. I will give one out of many examples of this.

In addition to the numerous memoirs published in connection with the disaster of the World War just ended, those of the Austrian statesman, Czernin, will soon appear. This book promises to be extremely interesting. It is difficult to express what I wish to say without the risk of being misunderstood; I mean that it is interesting because Czernin was a good deal less pretentious than the others who up to now have given expression to their opinions on the War, and he should therefore be leniently judged. In this book of Czernin's we may read something like the following passage:

> The War continues, though in another form. I believe that coming generations will not call this great drama, which has held the world in thrall for five years, the World War; they will call it the world revolution and they will know that the world revolution only began with the World War. Neither the Peace of Versailles nor that of St. Germain will create a lasting effect. This peace contains within it the destructive germ of death. The conflicts that shake Europe are not yet on the wane. As in a mighty earthquake, the subterranean rumbling still goes on. Now here, now there, the earth will continue to open and hurl fire towards heaven. Again and again events of elemental vehemence will sweep over the lands, bringing destruction in their train, till everything has been swept away, reminiscent of the madness of this War. Slowly, out of unspeakable sacrifice, a new world will be born. Coming generations will look back to our times as to a long, terrible dream. But the darkest night is followed by the dawn. Generations have sunk into graves, murdered, starved, victims of disease. Millions have died in the effort to annihilate, to destroy, their hearts filled with hatred and murder. But other generations will arise, and with them a new spirit. They will build up what war and revolution have destroyed. Every winter is followed by spring. It is an eternal law in the circuit of life that resurrection follows death. Happy those who are

called upon to co-operate as soldiers of labor in the work of rebuilding the world.

Even this man speaks of a new spirit, but this new spirit is only a shadowy conception, a dim presentiment in heads like his. In order that this new spirit may take hold of the hearts, of the minds, of the souls of men in a really concrete form, the spiritual science and the art of education of which I wished to speak today in connection with human evolution, will labor for the social future of humanity.

V

THE CO-OPERATION OF THE SPIRITUAL, POLITICAL AND ECONOMIC DEPARTMENTS OF LIFE FOR THE BUILDING UP OF A UNIFIED THREEFOLD SOCIAL ORGANISM.

In the second of this series of lectures I have sketched for you the method of constructing the spiritual, the political and the economic life. I have then endeavored in the succeeding lectures to describe in detail these three members of the body social and disentangle what has heretofore been considered a strict unity: All that relates to law, politics, and affairs of state should be administered in a democratic parliament. Everything relating to the spiritual and intellectual department of life should be detached from the political or equity state, and the spiritual organization should be independently administered in freedom. The economic organization, separated from the political and legal body, should form its own administration out of its own conditions and necessities, founded upon expert knowledge and technical capacity and skill.

Now the objection is always raised that such an arrangement of the social organism denies the necessity of building up social life as a unity. Every single institution, every separate work that can be achieved by the individual within the social organism, should endeavor to attain to such a unity, and this unity would be broken up, it is said, if any attempt were made to split the social organism into three parts.

This objection is quite reasonable and comprehensible, judged by the habits of thought of the present day, but, as we all see, it can by no means be justified. Yet is is comprehensible, because in the first place we need only glance at economic life itself in order to see how to the smallest details spiritual, political, and purely economic affairs overlap. In view of this state of things it may well be asked, "How could a splitting-up, a dismemberment, bring about any improvement?" Let us begin by taking the problem of the origin of merchandise, of actual commodities. We shall find that the value of a commodity, of merchandise, is already possessed of a threefold nature in that the commodity is produced, distributed, and consumed within the social organism; yet, as we shall see, this value gives the appearance of a unity bound to the commodity.

What determines the value of a commodity that can satisfy our requirements? In the first place we must have some personal need for the commodity in question. But let us examine how the need is determined. To begin with, it has, of course, to do with our bodily nature. For the bodily nature determines the value of the various material commodities. Even material goods are variously valued, according to the kind of education and requirements of the individual person, but where spiritual and intellectual products are concerned —and these are often inseparable from the sphere of the material, physical goods—we shall find that the method of valuing any commodity whatever is absolutely determined by the whole make-up of the human being, and the amount and kind of work he is willing to perform in order to possess that commodity. Here we see that it is the spiritual or intellectual element in man that determines the value of a commodity, or of any sort of merchandise.

Secondly, we see that the goods being exchanged between one man and another are limited by the conditions of ownership, and that means neither more nor less than that they are limited by legal conditions. Whenever one man tries to obtain a commodity from another, he touches in some way the other's rights to the commodity in question, so that economic life with its circulation of commodities is permeated throughout by all sorts of legal conditions.

In the third place, a commodity has not merely the value we attach to it through our requirements and the personal importance we give to these requirements, which is then transferred to the commodity; it has also an objective value in itself. It has an objective value to the degree that it is durable or the reverse, lasting or perishable; to the degree that by its nature it is more or less serviceable, plentiful, or scarce. All these things condition an objective, actual economic value, the determination of which demands an objective expert knowledge, and the production of which requires an objective technical capacity. But these three determinations of value are brought together into a unity in the commodity. Hence it may be asked with reason how what is united in the commodity can be separated and come under the administration of three departments, all concerned with the commodity and interested in its circulation.

Looking merely at the idea, it is certainly true that in life things can and do unite that are administered from the most diverse directions. On the one hand, why should not the subjective value that a man personally attaches to a commodity be determined by his education, which has its own independent administration? On the other hand, why should not legal conditions be given a place in the economic organization? Why should not all the objective value that

106

accrues to the commodity from expert knowledge and technical skill be added to the rest and unite in the object, in a unity? But all this is only idea and has no special value. What the threefold order of the social organism aims at in this direction must have a much deeper foundation. Here it must be said that the threefold order of the social organism is not an idea conceived out of personal inclinations by one or more persons; it is an impulse resulting from an impartial observation of the historical development of humanity in modern times. We may say that actually the most important impulses of humanity have been tending unconsciously in the direction of this threefold membering for centuries, only they have never gained sufficient force to carry it through. The failure to develop this force is the cause of the present state of things and of the misery in our surroundings. The time is ripe to say that the work must now be taken in hand for which preparation has been made for centuries; the work of bringing order into the social organism. The first thing we see is that the really free spiritual and intellectual life has broken away from the political and economic bodies, for the spiritual life that is dependent on the economic, legal-political organizations is by no means free. It is a portion of the spiritual life, torn away from the really fertile, free life of the spirit. It would be more exact to say that at the beginning of the period in which capitalism appeared with its division of labor on a grand scale, the really free spiritual life in certain spheres of art, philosophy, and religious conviction tore itself away from the economic organization and the political life, and was to a certain extent carried on unnoticed. That free spiritual life, forming only a part of all spiritual life, acts creatively only out of man's own impulses. In my lecture yesterday I claimed that freedom for the whole of spiritual life. Detached from the free spiritual life, which is the outcome of man's own impulses, exists all that man finds necessary for the administration of the economic life, and for the administration of law and order. What is necessary for the administration of economic affairs has become dependent upon the economic forces themselves. In the positions and circles in which economic power exists, the possibility also exists to train the next generation in economic science so that it may be able in its turn to attain economic power. But the science that has arisen out of economic life itself is only a part of all that might flow into the economic organization were the whole of spiritual life to be drawn upon for economic life. Actually, it is commercial risk alone, and everything resulting from it, that is made the object of study; this is worked up into a science of economics.

In regard to political life, the state requires functionaries and even learned men to fill its appointments, and these have been educated according to the stereotyped pattern prescribed for them by the state. The state, in its appointments, wishes and expects that qualities should be cultivated in individuals that can be used to its own advantage, but that brings about intellectual and spiritual enslavement even if a man imagines himself to be free. He is not aware of his dependence, does not see that he is confined within the limits of the stereotyped model held up to him. The truly free spiritual and intellectual life has won for itself a certain position in the world, independent of the economic and the political organizations. What is this position? I have already characterized it in part. That spiritual and intellectual life that has preserved its independence has become foreign to life; in one sense it has acquired an abstract character. We need only glance at the content of the philosophies of the free spiritual life, whether aesthetic, religious, or even scientific, in order to see that although much is said, it amounts to little more than admonitions to society. This content is there merely to appeal to the understanding and to feelings; it is there to play a part in the inner life of men, to fill the soul with inner comfort and well-being, but it has not the power or the impetus actually to enter and influence external life. Hence the unbelief in that spiritual life, to which I have already referred, proceeding from socialist quarters and expressed in the words, "No social idea however well-intended, if it is a purely spiritual one, can ever transform social life." To transform social life, real forces are necessary, but this abstract spiritual life is not reckoned as a real force. How far are the things that make up the inner life of the businessman or civil servant in his religion, or even his scientific convictions, removed from the laws he applies in business, in his position in life, in the administration of public affairs! It is absolutely a double outlook on life. On the one hand, principles that are entirely the outcome of economic and political life; on the other, a remnant of freedom, of spiritual life, condemned to impotence as regards inner affairs.

Thus it may be said that a unitary, free, spiritual life came into being centuries ago, but because this was not recognized in the ordering of public life, it has become abstract, devoid of reality. Now, because the influence of the spirit is needed in external social life, spiritual life reclaims its might, its power. That is the situation that now faces us. Political life has followed another direction. Whereas spiritual life has partly emancipated itself, the political organization has completely merged itself in the course of recent centuries in the powerful interests of the economic body. It has happened unnoticed, but in reality the two have become one. Economic interests and needs have found expression in public laws, and these are often held to be human rights. When scrutinized, however, they are found to be only economic and political interests and wants in the guise of laws. While, on the one hand, spiritual life demands its power, we find, on the other, that confusion has arisen in regard to the relation between legal and economic conditions. Large masses of the population throughout the civilized world include in their demands for the solution of the social problem a further fusion of the legal and economic organization. The whole of economic life is to be molded according to political and legal conceptions. If we examine today's favorite catchwords, what do we find but the last consequences of the fusion of political and economic life. We find that the radical socialist party, which influences wide circles of the population, demands that a political system, centralized, and graded as to administration, be tacked on to the economic life, and the economic life be hedged in on all sides by legal measures. The power of the law is to extend over economic processes.

This is the other aspect of the crisis that has arisen in our time, and we may say that through the demands for the increase of political and legal power over the economic life, tyranny of the state, of the legal system, over the economic system will arise. We see that the changes demanded for the recovery of economic life are not such as arise naturally out of economic conditions themselves; rather, this demand arises out of the quest for political power, which aims to take possession of and dominate economic life. Proletarian dictatorship—what is it but the last consequence of the fusion of legal and political with economic life.

Thus we see the necessity of thoroughly investigating the connection between law and politics, and the economic life at present. Free spiritual life has partly emancipated itself and demands restitution of its original powers, but if the legal system continues to be ever more closely bound up with the economic system, the whole social organism will be thrown into disorder. The subordination of thought to the suggestion that the state is a unity, and therefore the social body is also a unity, has lasted long enough. The time has now come for us to realize the consequence of that thought in the social chaos existing over a large part of the civilized world. Economic conditions demand complete separation from legal control because of the evident abuses that the political system would bring into economic affairs were the developments of the last centuries to be carried to their final consequence. The impulse of the threefold social organism takes cognizance of these facts, and I should like to give you a striking example of something that ought to work as a unity in life, but which is torn asunder owing to these very facts. It is said now that the aim of the threefold order is to break up the unity of social life. In the future, however, it will be said that the threefold order truly lays the foundation for that unity. A striking example will show us that an abstract endeavor to bring about unity has had just the effect of destroying unity. At present there are some superficial people who are extremely proud of the theoretic distinction they draw between law and morality. These people say that morality is the valuation of human action judged purely from the inner standpoint of the soul; that the judgment of an action, whether good or bad, is guided only by that inner standpoint, and precisely in questions of philosophy the moral judgment is carefully distinguished from the legal judgment, which belongs to outer, public life, and should be determined by the decrees and measures of political and social public life.

Of this separation of morality and law nothing was known up to the time of the rise of modern technical science and the later capitalism. Only within the last few centuries have the impulses of law and morality been torn asunder. Why? Because the moral judgment was diverted into that free spiritual life that has emancipated itself, but that has become powerless with regard to external life. The free spiritual life might be said to exist only for the purpose of exhortation or judgment. It has lost the power really to lay hold on life. Those maxims that might lay hold on life require economic impulses because they can no longer find purely human impulses, these having been relegated to the sphere of morality. These economic impulses are then turned into laws. Thus the activities of life, the determination of justice and the warmth infused into it by human morals are torn asunder. What ought to be a unity is torn apart into a duality.

A close study of the development of modern states will show that by insisting on the unitary character of the state, we have hastened the disunion of those very forces that should combine to produce a unity. The impulse of the three-membered social organism is in opposition to this separation. If we regard the actual principle of that impulse in its true light, we shall see there can be no question of any splitting up of life. The spiritual life should have its own administration. Has not every human being a connection with it, when it develops—as I have described it—in perfect freedom? Everybody is educated in that free spiritual life; our children are brought up in it; we find our immediate spiritual interests in it; we are united with it. The very people who are thus united with that spiritual life and draw their strength from it, are the very same people who live within the legal and political life, and determine the legal order governing their relations with one another. They establish that legal order by the help of the spiritual impulses that they take in from the spiritual life, and this legal order is the direct result of what has been acquired through contact with the spiritual life. Again, the tie that is developed, binding man to man democratically on the basis of the legal order, the impulse he receives as the basis of his relationship to other men, he carries into economic life, because there are again the same human beings who have a connection with the spiritual life, occupy a legal position, and carry on business. The measures the human being takes, the manner in which he associates with others, the way in which he transacts business, is all permeated with what he has developed in his spiritual life, and with the legal order he has established in economic life. They are the same men who work in the threefold organism and the unity is not effected by any abstract regulation, but by the living human beings themselves. Each member of the community, however, can develop his own nature and individuality in independence and can thus work for unity in the most effective manner. This applies to every member. We also can see how, under the suggestion of the state as the principal of unity, precisely what is inseparable in life becomes separated, even what is so intimately connected as law and morality.

Therefore the impulse to establish the threefold social organism is not to bring about the separation of what belongs together, but actually the co-operation of factors that ought to work together.

The spiritual life can only develop on its own free and independent basis. But when allowed to develop in this way, and granted an equal right to subsist side by side with the two other departments of the social organism, it will no longer be an abstract formation, like the spiritual life that has actually been developing for centuries apart from the realities of life. It will develop an impetus to play a direct part in the active, real life of the legal-political and the economic organizations. It might seem to be an absurd contradiction, a paradox, to assert that spiritual life should be fully independent and develop from its own foundations, as I showed yesterday, and also to claim that it shall play a part in the practical fields, but precisely when the spirit is left to itself does it develop impulses capable of embracing all spheres. For there is no reason why the free spirit in man should defer to any stereotyped pattern in the interest of the state. It is not to be limited by the condition that only those shall receive education who can command economic resources, but it will be able to develop human individuality in any generation through the observation of human capacities. The force, however, that strives to find expression in any one generation will not only embrace the phenomena and facts of nature. It will include, especially, human life itself because the spirit extends its interests over all life. We have been condemned to be unpractical in the sphere of spiritual matters because only these regions were left to the free spiritual life. We were denied the right to enter into external reality. As soon as the spirit is allowed not only to register parliamentary measures, but of itself to determine the laws of the state in freedom, in that moment it will make the legal code its own creation. The spirit will enter into the machinery and into the order of the law, as soon as the present mechanical system, which functions without thought according to certain maxims and points of view for the economic life, has been relinquished. As soon as the human spirit is free to play its part in the economic life it will at once prove its capacity in the practice of life within the economic circuit. All that is needed is to admit its power to enter actively into the practical realm. Then it will play its part. This true view of reality is a necessity. The spirit in man must not be hermetically sealed up in abstractions; it must be allowed to influence life. Then at every moment it will fructify the economic sphere, which otherwise must remain sterile, or must be dependent on mere chance for its fructification.

Now all this must be taken into account if we wish to arrive at a clear understanding of the manner in which the spiritual, the legal-political and the economic system should work together within the threefold social organism. There are clear-sighted persons to whom these things are still quite obscure. They often see that under present economic conditions, from which, we may say, the spirit has been banished, circumstances have arisen that are now socially untenable. There is, for instance, a highly respected economic thinker who holds the following opinion. He says that, looking at economic life today, what strikes us most is a system of consumption by which social evils are promoted in the highest degree. Those who possess the economic means today consume various things that are really only luxuries. He points out the role played by what he considers luxuries in the life of society and in economic life. Certainly this is not difficult. We need seek no further than the common occurrence of the purchase of a string of pearls by a lady. Many people would regard this as a harmless luxury. They do not consider the actual present economic value of a string of pearls. On the equivalent of its value, five working-class families can live for six months. Yet this is hung by the lady in question round her neck! Anybody can understand this, and in the present-day attitude of mind one can seek a remedy for such things. The esteemed thinker whom I have in mind thinks it necessary for the state (of course, everybody is now under the obsession of the state) to impose high taxes on luxuries, so high, indeed, that people would cease buying them. He does not admit the validity of the argument that if luxuries were taxed in this way, they would decrease, and the state then would lose the benefit of the taxation. He argues that this is just what should happen, and that the taxation has a moral aim. Taxation would then have the effect of promoting morality!

Such is the way of thinking today. So small is the belief in the power of the human spirit that it is proposed to establish the morality, which should spring from the human soul and spirit, by means of taxation, by law! No wonder that here, at any rate, no unity of life can be reached.

The same thinker points out that the acquisition of property is a wrong for the reason that monopolies are possible in our social life; that, for instance, social life still labors under the burden of the right of inheritance. Again he proposes to regulate all these things by taxation. If inherited property were taxed as highly as possible, he thinks that justice as regards property would result. It would also be possible to oppose monopolies and other evils of the same kind by law, by legal promulgations of the state. What strikes one in this thinker is that he says it is not of such importance that all these proposals should be determined by state laws, taxation, and so on, for it is plain that the value of such measures is by no means beyond dispute because state laws do not always produce the intended result. But then he says, "The essential point is not that these laws should actually raise the level of morality, or hinder monopolies; what matters are the feelings that prompt such laws."

This is an absolutely complete example of turning in a circle! A famous political thinker of our day does almost exactly the same thing. He proposes to call forth an ethical mode of thought and feeling by legislation, but, he says, it is not necessary that this legislation should actually be in force. The main thing is that people should have a feeling for such legislation. It is a clear case of the Chinaman who tries to catch himself by his own pigtail! It is a strange closing of the circle, but one that works most effectually in our present social life, for public life is now molded under the influence of this mode of thought. No one sees that all these things must lead in the end to the recognition of the fact that the basis for a really new construction of social life is the activity of the spiritual life in complete independence. Likewise, the independence of the

116

legal organization and its detachment from the economic system, and, finally, the untrammeled development of the economic organization.

Such things strike us forcibly today when we see how people, who are more than commonly well-intentioned, whose ethical sense for the need of a reconstruction of social life is beyond doubt, show at least a faint indication in their works of the absolute necessity for a spiritual foundation to the social edifice, and yet give evidence everywhere of a lack of understanding of the means by which that spiritual foundation can be attained.

Such a person is Robert Wilbrand, who has just written a book on the social problem. Robert Wilbrand is no mere theorist. In the first place, he speaks from a warm heart and enthusiasm for social things. Secondly, he has traveled all over the world in order to acquaint himself with social conditions, and in his book, which appeared a few weeks ago, he faithfully depicts the terrible misery of the human being that prevails everywhere today. He gives graphic pictures of the misery of the proletariat, the wretchedness of the civilized world. He shows also from his own standpoint how, in the most diverse regions in which the social question has now become acute, people have striven to build up a new social structure, but how they have been, or must be, frustrated, as may be plainly seen in today's Middle Europe (1919). Robert Wilbrand is quite certain that every attempt made in the temper of the present day must fail. Having given expression to this sentiment in various cadences in the course of his book, he concludes in the following remarkable manner. He says, "These attempts that are being made must fail; they will never succeed in any reconstruction because the social organism lacks a soul, and until it has a soul, it can accomplish no fruitful work." The most interesting part is that the book closes on

117

this note but does not indicate how this soul is to be found. The aim of the impulse for the threefold social organism is not to announce theoretically that the soul is lacking and wait till it appears of itself, but to point out how it will develop. It will develop when the spiritual life has been liberated from the political and economic organizations. The spiritual life, if it can only follow the impulses that man evolves from his spiritual nature, will then be strong enough to take its part in all the rest of practical life. Then spiritual life will take the form that I endeavored to describe yesterday; it will contain reality. We can say that in the present and in the future this spiritual life will be strong enough to bear the burden laid upon it that is mentioned in my book, *The Threefold Commonwealth*. It is true that we can now point out, as has been done in my second lecture, the way in which capital works today in the social economic process. But those who simply say that capital should be abolished or transformed into common property have no idea how capital works in the economic system, especially under the present conditions of production. They do not know that accumulations of capital are needed in order that through the control of capital men may work for the public good. For this reason in my book, *The Threefold Commonwealth*, the administration of capital was made, on the whole, dependent on the spiritual organization in co-operation with the independent political and legal organization. Whereas we now say that capital makes business, the impulse for the threefold order of the social organism requires that, although it should always be possible to accumulate capital, provision must be made for capital to be administered by someone who has developed out of the spiritual life the necessary capacity for business, and that this accumulation of capital may be administered by the person to whom it belongs only as long as he is able to administer it himself. When the capitalist can no longer put his own capacities into the administration of the capital, he must see—or if he should feel himself incapable of such a task, a corporation of the spiritual organization must assume the responsibility of seeing—that the management of the business shall pass to a highly capable successor, able to carry it on for the benefit of the community. That is to say that the transference of a business concern to any person or group of persons is not dependent on purchase or any other displacement of capital, but is determined by the capacity of individuals themselves. It is a matter of transfer from the capable to the capable, from those who can work in the service of the community to those who can also work in the best way for the common good. On this kind of transference the social safety of the future depends. It will not be an economic transference, as is now the case; this transference will result from the impulses of the human being, received from the independent spiritual-intellectual life and from the independent legal-political life. There will even be corporations within the cultural organization, united with all other departments of the cultural life, on which the administration of capital will devolve.

Thus, instead of handing over the means of production to the community, we transfer it from one capable person to another equally capable, that is, the means of production is circulated within the community. This circulation depends on the freedom of the cultural life by which it is effected and upheld. So we may say that the main factor in the circuit of economic life is the impulse at work in the spiritual and in the equity life. It would be impossible to imagine any unity more complete than that effected in economic life by such measures. But the stream that unites itself with the economic organization flows from the free spiritual and the free political organizations. No longer will society be exposed to the chance that is expressed in supply and demand, or in the other factors in our present economic organization. Reasonable and just relations between man and man will enter into this new economic life, so that the spiritual, legal and economic organizations will work together as one, even though they are administered separately. Man will carry over from one sphere into another—since he belongs to all three—what each one needs. It is true that we must free ourselves from many a prejudice if these things are gradually to be brought to pass. Today we are absolutely convinced that the means of production and land are matters belonging to economic life. The impulse of the threefold order requires that only the reciprocal values of things shall come under the economic administration, and that prices shall approximate values, so that ultimately what finally proceeds from the economic administration is merely the determination of price.

It is impossible to reach a just determination of price as long as the means of production and land function as they now do within the economic system. The disposal of land, systematized in the laws relating to its ownership, and the disposal of the finished means of production (for example, a factory with its machinery and equipment), should be no matter for the economic organization. They must belong partly to the spiritual and partly to the legal. That is to say, the transference of land from one person or group of persons to another must not be carried out by purchase or through inheritance, but by transference through legal means, on the principles of the spiritual organization. The means of production through which something is manufactured—a process that lies at the basis of the creation of capital—can only be looked at from the point of view of its commodity-cost while it is being built up. Once it is ready for operation, the creator of it takes over the management because he understands it best. He has charge of it as long as he can personally use his capacities. But the finished means of production is no longer a commodity to be bought and sold. It can only be transferred by one person or group of persons to another person or group of persons by law, or rather, by spiritual decisions confirmed by law. Thus, what at present forms part of the economic life, such as the laws relating to the disposal of property, to the sale of land, and to the right of disposal of the means of production, will be placed on the basis of the independent legal organization working in conjunction with the independent spiritual organization. These ideas may appear strange and unfamiliar today, but this fact is just what is so sad and bitter. Only when these things find entrance into the minds and souls and hearts of men, so that the human being orders his social life accordingly, only then can be fulfilled what so many try to bring about in other ways, but always without success.

A truth that must now at last be recognized is that much, which at present appears paradoxical, will seem a matter of course when social life is really on the way to recovery.

The impulse for the three-membered social organism makes no social demands on the basis of passion, or impelled by motives and emotions that often underlie these social demands. It puts forward its demands from a study of the actual recent evolution of humanity right up to the present day. It sees how, in the course of long centuries, one form of social life has given place to another. Let us go back to a time before the end of the Middle Ages. We find a condition of things extending into the latter part of medieval times, especially in civilized Europe. We find society in a condition that we may call a social order of might. This society of might or despotism arose in the following way, to give one example of the manner in which such changes are brought about. Some conqueror, with his train of followers, settled in some locality and these became his workmen. Then, since the leader was looked up to on account of his individual qualities, his abilities, a social relationship was brought about between his power and that of those whom he had once led, and who afterwards became his servants or his workmen. Here the model for the social organism, which took its rise in one person or in one aristocratic group, passed on to the community at large, and lived on in that community. The will of the community was to a certain extent only the reproduction or the projection of the single will in that society of might, of despotism.

Under the influence of modern times, of the division of labor, of capitalism, of technical culture, this despotic order of society gave place to the system of trade, of exchange, which, however, carries on the same impulses among individuals and in the whole life of the community. The commodity produced by the individual becomes merchandise, which is exchanged for something else. For financial economy is, in reality, so far as it consists in a transaction between individuals or groups, neither more nor less than a system of trading. Social life is a system of trading. Whereas under the old despotic system, the whole community had to do with the will of a single individual, which it accepted, the system of trading under which we are still living and from which a great part of the population of the world is striving to extricate itself, has to do with the will of one individual opposed to the will of another. Only out of the co-operation of one single member with another arises, as if by chance, the collective will of the community. Springing from intercourse between one individual and another the economic community takes shape, together with wealth, and the element we recognize in plutocracy. In all this there is something at work that has to do with the clashing of individual interests with one another. It is no wonder that the old despotic order of society could not aspire to the smallest emancipation of the spiritual life, for on account of his superior capacity their leader was also recognized as the authority in the spiritual, and in the legal order. But it is quite comprehensible that the legal, the state, the political principle has gained the upper hand, especially in the trading system of society. Have we not seen on what foundation law actually wills to rest, even though that will does not find its true expression in the present social order?

Law is really concerned with all that the individual man has to regulate with other individual men who are his equals. The trading system is an order in which one person has to do with another. It was, therefore, to the interest of the society based on the trading system to transform its economic system, in which one person has to do with another, into a legal system; that is to say, to change economic interests into legal statutes. Just as the old despotic system was transformed into a society of trading, this latter system now strives, out of the innermost impulses of human evolution, to take a new social form, especially in the domain of economics. The system of trading, having appropriated to itself the spiritual life, having enslaved it and turned it away from real life, has gradually grown into a mere economic system of society, the form demanded by certain radical socialists. But, out of the deepest human impulses of our day, this trading system strives to pass, especially in the domain of economic life, into that form which I might call, even if the term is inadequate, the Commonwealth. The society of traders must be transformed into the commonwealth.

What form will the Commonwealth take? Just as the individual will, or the will of an aristocracy, which is also a kind of individual will, continues in a sense to work in the whole community, so that the impulses of the individuals only represent an extension of the will of the one; just as the trading system had to do with the clashing of one individual will with another, so the economic order of the Commonwealth will have to do with a kind of collective will, which then in reverse fashion works back on the individual will. I explained in the second lecture how associations of the various branches of production with the consumers will be called into existence in the sphere of economic life, so that everywhere there will be a combination of the producers with the consumers. These associations will enter into contracts with other associations. A kind of collective will then arises within larger or smaller groups. This collective will is an ideal for which many socialists yearn, but they visualize the matter in a confused, by no means reasonable, manner. Just as in the society of despotism, of power, the single will worked in the community, so there must work in the future Commonwealth a common will, a collective will.

How will that be possible? As we know, it must arise through the co-operation of single wills. The single wills must give a result that is no tyranny for the individual, but within which everyone must be able to feel himself free. What must be the content of this collective will? In it must be contained what every soul and every human body can accept, something with which they are in agreement, with which they can grow familiar. That means that the spirit and soul living in the individual human being must also live in the collective will of the Commonwealth. This is possible only when those who build up the collective will carry in themselves of their own will, in their intentions, in their feelings and in their thoughts, a complete understanding of the individual man. Into that collective will must flow all that is felt by the individual man, as his own spiritual, moral, and bodily nature. This is imperative.

This was not so in the society of might, which acted instinc-

124

tively, in which a single person was looked up to by the community, because the individual persons forming the community could not make their individual will felt. Nor was it so in the trading system of society, in which a single individual will clashed with others, and a chance kind of common life arose from it. It must be otherwise when an organized collective will influences the individual. Then, no one who shares in the forming of that collective will must lack understanding of what is truly human. There no one who is equipped only with abstract modern science, which applies merely to external nature, and which can never explain the whole man, must presume to decide questions on the philosophy of life. Men will approach the philosophy of life with spiritual science, which embraces the whole man, body, soul, and spirit, and provides understanding in regard to the feeling and will of every single person. Hence, it will only be possible to establish an economic order of the community, when the economic organization can be inspired by the independent spiritual life. It will thus not be possible to bring about a sound future unless what is thought in the free life of the spirit is reflected back from the economic life. That free spiritual life will not prove itself unpractical, but on the contrary, prove itself very practical. Only he who lives in an atmosphere of spiritual slavery can be content just to reflect on good and evil, on the true and the false, the beautiful and the ugly within his own soul. But anyone who, through spiritual science, has learned to behold the spirit as a living force, and who grasps it by the aid of spiritual science, will be practical in all his actions, especially in everything relating to human life. What he absorbs from his spiritual vision passes immediately into every function of life; it actually puts on a form that enables it to live in the immediate practice of life. Only a spiritual culture that has been banished from practical life can become foreign to life. A spiritual culture that is allowed to influence practical life develops in the practice. He who really knows what spiritual life is, knows how close to practical life that spirit element is when it is allowed to follow its own impulses unhindered. The man who desires to found a new philosophy, and who does not know even how to chop wood should the occasion arise, is no really good philosopher. He who would found a philosophy, without the ability to turn his hand to anything in the direct practice of life, can found no philosophy of life, but only one foreign to all life. True spiritual life is practical. Under the influences that have made themselves felt for centuries, it is comprehensible that there should be persons belonging to the present civilization—among them the leaders of our intellectual life—who are of the same opinion as Robert Wilbrand. In his book on social reconstruction he says with the best intentions and from a feeling prompted by true ethics: "No practical work of reconstruction can be accomplished because the soul is lacking." But people cannot bring themselves to ask about the reality of soul-development, of soul-building; they cannot make up their minds to ask, "What is the effect of a truly free spiritual life on the political and economic life?" That free spiritual life will, as I have shown, rightly co-operate with the economic life. Then the economic life, which can co-operate with the political and spiritual life, can at all times train men who will in their turn give stimulus to the spiritual life. Through the three-membered social organism a free, absolutely real life of the community will be brought about. Then those persons who now, out of instinct rather than out of a true courage in life, seek a vague something that they call soul or spirit, may be answered in these words, "Learn to recognize the reality of your spiritual nature. Give to the spirit the things of the spirit, and to the soul the things of the soul, and it will then be plain also what belongs to the economic life."

VI

NATIONAL AND INTERNATIONAL LIFE
IN THE THREEFOLD SOCIAL ORGANISM.

It is quite possible that to some among my audience my manner of dealing with the subject of these lectures may have appeared somewhat singular. Singular, inasmuch as it might possibly be said that these are isolated ideas and thoughts on a possible way of building the social structure, and that the catchwords so common in the social movements of today are noticeably lacking in these lectures. Certainly, thoughts and ideas must be a foundation, but I think it has been made clear that these thoughts and ideas differ considerably from much else that has been said on the subject. For instance, we often hear it said that there is no equal distribution of wealth, and that some evil is the cause of this; that such evils must be abolished, and so on. We often hear such remarks today. It appears to me more important to act in this sphere just as in practical life. If we have to do with some commodity needed by human beings, and produced by a machine, it is not enough to draw up a program and announce that a meeting must be called and an organization founded in order that the commodity in question may be produced. This is the way modern social programs come into being. It seems to me far more important to indicate the way in which the machine, in the present instance the *social organism,* should be put together and utilized in order that it bring forth something that will meet the more or less conscious social demands of the present day.

I think no one can say that these lectures have not dealt with the means by which bread, coal, or other necessities are produced. In my opinion they have dealt with such matters. They have dealt with the actual foundations of the social organism, with the manner in which men must live and work together within that social organism in order to bring about the fulfillment of social demands. I wish to preface my lecture with these remarks because such a reproach might possibly be made in regard to this, my concluding lecture.

Only those who see why the price of bread that appears on every table is connected with the economy of the entire world, and why the events taking place in Australia or America and the commodities these countries produce are related to the price paid here for bread or coal, will recognize the presence of an international problem that involves the whole social question. In view of the many prevailing opinions and prejudices, however, it is not exactly easy to speak of the international problem at the present moment. Have we not seen to what unheard-of conditions international intercourse has led us during the last five years? Did not the belief prevail within the widest circles—pre 1919—that international feeling, international understanding had been established in modern humanity? To what has this international feeling, this international understanding led? It has led to the fact that over a large part of the civilized world the people have torn one another to pieces! Even those ideas and idealistic aims whose greatest value lay in their international character have proved a failure, as their promoters themselves acknowledge. We need only recall the words, the pronouncements and views of international Christianity, for this is what it claimed to be, as it joined in so many cases in the chorus of international chauvinism. We might cite many instances of the shipwrecking of international impulses in late years. Also, when we speak of the international life of mankind, perhaps more particularly in reference to its economic aspect, we shall find it necessary to revise our thoughts and our judgments in this respect. It will be necessary to penetrate to these sources of human nature, which can only be found when we look towards the spirit and the soul. To do so, to avoid the mere repetition of the words 'spirit' and 'soul,' to give heed instead to the actual dominance of the spirit and soul, this, in my opinion, has at least been attempted in these lectures.

All over the world the relations existing among human beings in their common work are governed by two impulses, about which it is of the highest importance that the truth should prevail among us, a true unvarnished conception, not disfigured by hackneyed phrases. Two impulses dwell in the human soul, which are related just as the north and south poles of a magnetic compass are related to one another. These two impulses are *egoism* and *love*. It is a widespread opinion that ethical law requires that egoism be conquered by love, and that in the progress of human evolution pure love should supplant egoism. This claim is put forward by many on the ground of ethics, and today also as a social need, but an understanding of the kind of opposition that actually exists between the two forces of egoism and love is certainly less evident in our day. In speaking of egoism, we should recognize that it begins with the bodily needs of the human being. We cannot understand what arises from the bodily needs of the human being unless we regard it as belonging to the sphere of egoism. The needs of the human being proceed from egoism. Now we must believe that it is possible to ennoble the feeling of egoism and, therefore, it is not a good thing to form one's opinions from the phrases current on this subject. To say that egoism must be overcome by love does not help us much to understand egoism. For the point is, that he who meets his fellow men with a purely human interest and understanding acts differently from one whose interests are narrow, and who gives no thought to all that fills the hearts and souls of his fellow creatures, and who is without interest for his surroundings. On this account, the former, who is truly interested in his fellow men, need not be less egoistic in life than the other because his egoism may be precisely his desire to serve human beings. It may call forth in him a feeling of inner well-being, of inner bliss, even of ecstasy, to devote himself to the service of his fellow men. Then, as far as the outer life is concerned, deeds that are absolutely altruistic to all appearance may proceed from egoism; in the life of feeling they cannot be appraised otherwise than as egoism.

But the question of egoism must be extended much further. We must follow it through the whole life of the human soul and spirit. We must see clearly how the spirit and soul nature arise out of man's inner being in various manifestations, just as the bodily wants arise. Thus, everything in the nature of creative fantasy, of imaginative creation arises out of the inner being; likewise all creations in the sphere of art. If we proceed in our investigations without bias and seek a right understanding of such things, we shall find the creator of man's imagination. All that rises out of the unknown depths of his being has the same source, but at a higher stage than the bodily wants. The life of imagination, of fantasy, which is developed in art, viewed subjectively, reposes on a feeling of inward satisfaction, more refined, nobler than the satisfaction of hunger, for instance, but not different in quality for the individual himself, even if what is produced thereby may have a different significance for the world.

All human egoism is directed by the fact that man must agree with his fellows, that he should live and work together with them. Egoism itself requires that he should live and work with other men. Much of what we carry out in common with other men is absolutely founded on egoism, and still may be credited to the noblest human virtues. If we contemplate maternal love, we find that it is absolutely founded on the egoism of the mother; yet it manifests itself most nobly in the common life of humanity.

What is actually founded on egoism, because man needs his fellow men for egoistic reasons, extends over the common family life, over the common life of the tribe, over the common life of the nation, of the people, and the manner in which a man conducts himself among his people and in his nation is nothing but the reflection of his own egoism. In the love of country, in patriotism, egoism doubtless rises to a high level; it is ennobled; it takes the form of an ideal and rightly so, but that ideal is, nevertheless, rooted in human egoism. Now this ideal must spring from human egoism, and it must be realized in order that the productivity of a people may be able to pass on something to humanity. So we see how from that single impulse of the human soul—egoism, all that ultimately finds expression in nationalism is developed. Nationalism is egoism experienced by the whole nation in common. Nationalism is egoism carried into the spiritual region of life. Nationalism, for instance, is saturated with, glows with, the imagination of the people in which it finds expression. But this life of imagination itself is the higher spiritual development of all that constitutes human wants. We must go back to this root, in order to gain a clear understanding of it by right contemplation.

Of a different species is that characteristic of human nature that develops as internationalism. We become national, because the feeling of nationalism arises out of our own nature. Nationalism is a blossom on the growth of the individual human being who is of the same blood as his tribe, or is bound by other ties to his people. Nationalism grows with the man. It grows into him as a certain bodily growth. He does not possess internationalism in this way. Internationalism is rather comparable to the feeling we acquire when we contemplate the beauties of nature; through this contemplation we are impelled to love, to reverence, to understanding, because it has become a reality to us, because it impresses itself on us, because we give ourselves up to it freely. Whereas we grow into our own nation because we are, so to speak, members of it, we learn to know other nations. They work on us indirectly through our knowledge of them, our understanding of them. We learn little by little to love them with understanding, and in proportion to our learning to love and to understand mankind in its different peoples in their various countries, does our feeling grow for internationalism. There are two absolutely distinct sources in human nature from which arise, respectively, nationalism and internationalism. Nationalism is the highest development of egoism. Internationalism is what permeates us more and more as we give ourselves to a wide understanding of human nature. We must regard the common life of human beings all over the civilized globe in this light, especially if we wish to come to a clear understanding of the conflicting element in these impulses, nationalism and internationalism.

Even if the economic life were governed by its own conditions, and an attempt were made to understand it, it would still be necessary to point to the two impulses in the human soul just mentioned. What we have called the threefold human life element in these lectures leads us back to these two impulses in the human soul. Think of the economic system, for instance; consider how it pervades the whole national and international life of humanity. Let us examine this economic system. We are compelled to recognize its origin in human wants, in consumption. The satisfaction of these wants is really the whole task of economic life. Production and distribution of commodities, administration, human intercourse, and so on, are necessary to supply human requirements. Here again we may ask what element of human nature lies at the root of requirement, of consumption. Egoism is at their root. It is important that this fact should be properly understood. If it is understood, no one will feel impelled to ask with regard to the economic life, "How can we overcome egoism?" but rather, "How is it possible for altruism to meet the just demands of egoism?" Perhaps this question may sound less idealistic, but it is the true one.

When we turn our attention to production by which consumption is satisfied, we see at once that something else is necessary. The producer is of course at the same time the consumer. He whose business it is to produce must have an understanding not only of the process of production, but also of the life of his fellow men, so that he can devote himself to the work of production in a manner corresponding to their needs. The producer must be able, indirectly or directly through institutions of which we have spoken, to see what men need for their consumption. He must then devote himself unselfishly and with understanding to some kind of production for which he has the capability. It is only necessary to describe this, and people will be forced to see that the real motive power of production is self-sacrificing love towards human society, even though the sphere in which it manifests may appear dry and uninteresting. Nothing constructive will ever be said regarding the actual solution of the social problem until it is understood that production can only be regulated in a social manner by the creation, through the spiritual and equity organizations, of a source from which unselfish love for the various branches of production can flow into the human soul, because of the producers' interest in their fellow men and in life.

Between these two—consumption governed by egoism, and production in which love is the ruling principle—there is the distribution of commodities, holding the balance between them. Today this is brought about through the rise and fall of the market, through supply and demand, but in future times an association of men will substitute intelligence for the fluctuation of the market. Men will be there who will make it their task to regulate production in conformity with their observation of the needs of the consumer. So that the market will consist in commodities that the associations, already mentioned, will be able to produce, these associations having first studied and observed intelligently the needs of consumption. All catchwords in this department of life will be discarded, and the attention will be given wholly to realities. Who has not seen that in modern times something has arisen that was bound to appear as a result of the continual widening of man's horizon all over the world? Instead of the former national economy, limited to small territories, we have a world economy. It is true that so far this world economy is only in the stage of a sort of demand, though it has developed to such an extent that in almost every part of the world commodities are consumed that are produced in other parts of the world. Here again human ideals and the feelings of the human soul have not kept pace with the world requirements that have become evident. Everywhere we see how urgent is the demand of modern times for a world economy, for arrangements by which a world economy could be rendered possible.

What are the conditions under which world economy is alone possible? Of a truth, this question can only be answered after we have first turned our attention to the form that the social order of the future must take from the present time on, if the order of the Commonwealth takes the place of the old despotic order—that of might—and of the present method of trade. The Commonwealth is the social order in which production will be carried on by associations, through contracts with other associations.

If this should really come about, where would the real difference lie between such a community, and the mere trading system of society, the ruling system today?

The difference shows itself in the fact that in the trading system the individual or the single group has, for the most part, to do with another individual or another group. What are the common interests of individuals or groups in their mutual relations? At present, whether they are producers or consumers, their production and consumption are divided from one another, as if by a chasm, by the chances of the market. The chances of the market are the means of bringing about the distribution of commodities and of facilitating commerce. Whatever may be our opinion as to the justification or otherwise of the domination of capital, or of labor, and the like, that is, as to the significance of capital and the significance of labor, it must be admitted that the essential fact in our system of exchange is that the distribution of commodities should be the ruling factor. Distribution is the link between production and consumption;

when these are sundered from each other by the abyss of the market, there is no means of communication between them through the exercise of intelligence.

What will take the place in the Commonwealth of the system of distribution now prevailing? The whole domain of economic life will be drawn into the sphere of interest of every producer. Whereas it is now the interest of the producer to find out how he can procure and dispose of his products, which, however, he does out of self-interest, it will be necessary for every producer in the Commonwealth to have a full interest in consumption, distribution, and production. That is to say, it will be necessary that the entire economic process be reflected in the economic interests of the individual man. This must be the essential point in the social order of the Commonwealth.

Let us see what would be the position of this Commonwealth, which also in the single state today is undoubtedly a demand of the future, with regard to the international problem. How does this international problem present itself to us, especially with regard to the economic system? We can see that though a universal demand exists for a world economy, the single nations stand separate within the circuit of the whole world economy. These separate nations, apart from the other historical causes of their existence, are held together for a time by the feelings arising out of the egoism of the community. Even in the highest part of the life of a nation, in literature, art, science, religion, it is the imagination arising out of egoism that holds the groups of people together. The groups thus held together take their place in the sphere of world economy, and in the course of the nineteenth century they have asserted themselves with particular energy, and ever more decidedly up to the beginning of the twentieth century, when the climax was reached. We

136

might describe what really happened by saying that while other interests, which bore a much greater resemblance to those of the old despotic order of society, formerly prevailed between the nations, the principle of exchange and barter became even more prominent, precisely in the mutual intercourse of nations. This condition of things, therefore, reached its height at the beginning of the twentieth century. Just as production and consumption were carried on in the various states, so what was supplied to other states or was derived from them was absorbed into the egoism of the various states. Thus value was attached only to that in which the single state, as a nation, was interested. The reciprocal economic relations established between the states were absolutely dependent upon the commercial principle ruling the system of trade in regard to the distribution of commodities. In this sphere but on a large scale, it was especially evident how the mere system of trade must lead ad absurdum, and the fact that this actually came to pass was one of the chief causes that led to the disaster of the World War.

That this great opposition existed between the demand for a world economy and the influence of the various states against its realization is now becoming ever more evident. Instead of promoting a world economy, these states closed their frontiers, shut themselves off by imposing customs and duties and by other measures, and laid claim to every advantage that might result from a world economy, seizing all for themselves. This led to the crisis we call the catastrophe of the World War. There were, of course, other causes of the disaster, but this is one of the chief causes. Therefore it is important to understand that the very first step towards the improvement of international relations is to be able to carry on commerce across frontiers, but on different principles from those on which the present system of exchange is based.

Just as every single person, if he wishes to share in the work of the community, must take an interest in production and consumption wherever it is carried on, just as every member of the community must be interested in the whole sphere of economy, consumption, production and distribution, so in every country in the world impulses must prevail that would lead to a genuine interest in every other country. Thus nothing resembling the chance conditions of the present market could prevail among the peoples of the earth, but a real inner understanding would prevail among them.

Here we come to the deeper sources of what is being sought through the abstract ideals of the so-called League of Nations, the avowed object of which is the correction of certain evils in the common life of nations. But the principle underlying it is the same as that on which many other schemes are now founded. Many of those who today ponder over the evils of life seize upon the first means at hand to carry out some reform or other. Someone sees that a certain luxury has wide distribution and feels impelled to impose a tax on it, and so forth. Such a reformer never thinks of going to the source of the evil in question, of devising a social structure for the community in which an undesirable luxury could not come into existence, but this is precisely what is necessary in the life of nations. Therefore, we shall never attain sincere international social relations by regulations of a merely corrective character. There is no other way than by finding the source of a common understanding among the various peoples.

There can be no understanding of other nations as long as we keep to one thing that is as natural to the human being as his growth, so long as we look only to what must lead to nationalism, to the division of peoples among themselves. What is there in the spiritual life of our day that is the only thing that bears an international character, and alone has not been lost during the War because it was impossible for men to take this character away from it? Had this been done, the field itself would have been annihilated. What is there that is truly international on the earth? Nothing but the field of modern science, which is concerned only with the outer world of the senses.

Abstract science has acquired an international character. It has been easy to see in these times, when there has been so much falsehood in the world, that, whenever anybody did science the injury of misusing it in the service of nationalism, he robbed it of its true character. Do we not see by this fact also that this kind of spiritual life that expresses itself in intellectualism was not able to establish international understanding? I think it may be seen clearly enough that the powerlessness of this abstract trend of thought, which I have described from so many different points of view, has shown itself most distinctly in the relation of this abstract spiritual life to internationalism. Science was not able to pour into the human soul international impulses deep enough to resist the terrible influences of these last years. Where science attempted to evoke social impulses, such as those in the international socialist movement, it was found that international socialism was also unable to hold its own, and that it mostly flowed away into national channels. Why did this happen? Just because from among the old heirlooms of humanity it had only inherited intellectuality, and intellectuality is not powerful enough to work creatively in life. Thus we see how this new scientific mode of thought, which arose simultaneously with capitalism and technical science, contains within it an international element, and yet at the same time proves its impotence to establish a true international relationship among men. In contrast to this, we must call to mind and apply here what I said in my fourth lecture re-

139

garding the mode of thought known as spiritual science, which is founded on perception and knowledge of the spirit.

This spiritual perception does not rest on outer sense perception; it is the result of the individual development of human nature. It springs from the same soil as imagination, but it is rooted in profounder depths of human nature. For this reason it rises not only to subjective, imaginative forms, but reaches to the objective knowledge of the realities of the spiritual world. This kind of spiritual perception is today often misunderstood. Those who have no knowledge of it say what can be found in this way by spiritual perception is merely subjective, and cannot be proved. Mathematical truths are also subjective and incapable of being proved! No agreement among individuals can confirm the truths of mathematics. Anyone acquainted with the Pythagorean theorem knows that it is true, even if a million others contradict it. Thus, spiritual science is also presented as an objective aim. It takes the same way as imagination, and rises higher; it is rooted in the objective depths of human nature, and ascends to objective heights. Hence this spiritual perception rises above all that, which as imagination, inspires the nations. It is sought equally by one people or another, in one language or another. It is one and the same in the experience of all human beings all over the earth if it is only sought deeply enough. Hence the spiritual perception that, as I have indicated, can actually enter into and inform practical social life, can, at the same time, enter actively into international life and form a bond of union between one people and another. The poetry of a people, its peculiarities in other branches of art, will be produced by it in its own individual way. To spiritual perception something arises out of the individuality of a people that is similar to what arises elsewhere. The roots from which things spring are in various places. The final source of all results is the same over the whole earth. Many people speak of the spirit today who do not know that the spirit must be interpreted. When the spirit is understood, it is found to be something that does not separate, but unites men, because it can be traced back to the inmost being of man, and because one human being brings forth the same as another, and because he fully understands that other.

When we actually spiritualize what otherwise finds expression as individualism in the imagination of one people, the single peoples will become simply the manifold expression of what, to spiritual perception, is one. Then, over the whole earth, people will find it possible to tolerate the different national peculiarities because there will be no need for an abstract uniformity everywhere; the concrete one, found through spiritual perception, will find means of expression in manifold ways. By this means the many will be able to understand each other in the spiritual unity. Then, from the many kinds of understanding of the unity, they will be able to frame articles for a League of Nations, and then, out of the spiritual conditions, out of the spiritual understanding, legal statutes can arise that will unite the nations. Then in the individual peoples will appear what is possible to every people, namely, interest in the production and consumption carried on by other peoples. Then through the spiritual life, the legal and judicial life of the peoples, one nation will really be able to develop an understanding of other nations and peoples over the whole earth.

People must make up their minds to recognize the spirit in this department of life, or they will be obliged to renounce all hope of bringing about any improvement, no matter how well-intentioned their statutes may be. It is true, large numbers of people now express their disbelief in the working of this spiritual element; this is comprehensible, because they have not the courage to approach this spiritual truth. It is truly hard for the spirit to gain a hearing, but when it can unfold, even in a small circle in spite of hindrances, it shows itself to be all that I have just said of it. If only the feelings of the people in some of the belligerent states could have been known, if their thoughts about their enemies, their hatred towards each other, could have been seen, and the absence of international feeling existing in the countries at war been realized, you would understand why I returned again and again to the place I have already mentioned in these lectures, in northwest Switzerland, where spiritual science has erected the Goetheanum, the University of Spiritual Science.

What sort of place was that during the years of the War? It was a place where, during the whole War, people of all nations worked together without intermission, without any lessening of understanding each other, in spite of many a discussion that may or may not have been necessary. This mutual understanding, since it was the result of a common grasp of a spiritual conception of life, has already become a reality, even though for the present only in a small circle. We may say that we have been able to make the experiment in this sphere. We have been able to show that those who met there from time to time were able to understand others. This understanding must not be sought by vague allusions to the spirit. It must be sought through the most intense, sincere self-conquest, by means of the impulse of the spirit. Men and women of today do not wish to hear that the spirit must be striven for by each one personally. There is much talk nowadays about the spirit, that the spirit must come and must permeate the purely materialistic social demands, but, beyond this appeal to the spirit, we hear little! If such people, who in other respects are well-meaning, full of insight and permeated by social ethics, would only reflect that we have indeed had

142

the spirit! Can we appeal today to that same spirit that has been with us? It is that very spirit that has brought us into our present circumstances. Therefore, what we want is not a new situation created by the old spirit. An old spirit cannot bring us anything new! This has been proved to us. We need a new spirit. We must strive for this new spirit and it can only be won in an independent spiritual life. Therefore, if we picture to ourselves how the demand for a world economy will be fulfilled—for fulfilled it will be, out of its own inner necessity—we shall find that within its scope one social form will take its place beside another, everywhere producing spiritual and legal conditions out of the human beings who live together in those social bodies. What is brought forth in this individual manner will be precisely the means for the understanding of other social bodies, and will thus become the means by which true world economy will be carried on. Unless such means are created, the old so-called national interests will arise again and again in world economy, and will claim for themselves all that they can extract. As every social body has the same desire and will be void of understanding for the others, disharmony must of necessity again make its appearance. How, then, can a world economy be carried on? Only in so far as political and intellectual organizations do not dominate the individual forms of the economic system, for they must have an individual form. They attain universality and unity in spiritual understanding alone, which over the whole earth is the other unity. In order that the earth may be freed from individualism that other unity must be everywhere recognized.

Even as it is true that, if we only descend deeply enough into human nature, we may develop to objective heights in which we find, as a spiritual perception, what may also be found by anyone of any other nation, so it is also true that the needs of human consumption all over the earth are not affected by variations in nationality. Human wants are international, only they are the opposite pole of what is spiritually international. The internationality of the spirit must furnish the understanding, must permeate with love that understanding of other nationalities, and must be able to expand that love to internationalism in the sense already indicated. Egoism is equally international. Internationalism will only be able to establish a connection with world production when the latter springs from a common spiritual understanding, from a common spiritual conception of unity. Never out of the egoism of the peoples will understanding of universal consumption arise. From a universal spiritual perception alone can that develop that proceeds not from egoism, but from love, and that, therefore, can govern production. What is the cause of the demand for world economy? Owing to the growing complexity in the conditions of human life everywhere, and the consequent increasing similarity of human needs, it becomes ever more evident that human beings everywhere have the same wants.

How can a uniform principle of production be created to meet this uniform demand, one that will actively promote a world economy? It can be created through our upward striving to the spiritual life, to a true spiritual perception, which is powerful enough to create a common world production for the common world consumption. Then the balance can be struck, because unity in the spirit will work towards unity of consumption, towards unity of substance. Then the balance will be struck in the distribution of goods as mediator between production and consumption. Thus we must be able to look into the human soul, if we would understand how, over the whole civilized world—in reality out of many organisms—one uniform organism may arise. In no other way can this uniform organ-

144

ism be built up, this uniform organism that must be such that, in accordance with social demands all over the world, a true organic bond may be created between production and consumption, so that the piece of bread, or the coal required for the single household, or for the single person, may truly correspond with the social demands that are now making themselves felt in the subconsciousness of the human race.

I know very well that when such subjects are raised to this sphere of observation, many will say that this is the height of sheer idealism! Nevertheless, in that sphere alone is to be found the impelling force for manifold things outside that sphere. It is just because men have not sought that driving force, which can only be found in this way, that the present social and political conditions now prevail over the whole civilized world. People must come to realize that those who make it their task to create the inner impelling forces for the single social organism, such as the state, and for the social organism of the world, are the truly practical workers. They must come to see that many workers who are often called "practical" have only a rudimentary and merely abstract knowledge of their true sphere. Not until these two facts are recognized will the social question be placed on a healthy foundation.

One of those to whom all this has been a matter of most serious thought for a long time, when he was lecturing on a particular aspect of human life, pointed out that the so-called idealists are by no means the most ignorant concerning the connection of ideals with real life. He was conscious of the folly of those who call themselves practical, and who consider that the thoughts of the idealist are beautiful, but that practical life demands something quite different. The truth is that practicality actually demands these ideals, if it is ever to become true practicality. The would-be practical people hinder the realization of these ideals because they are either too lazy to understand them or have an interest in preventing their realization. The same man of whom I have spoken said, "The idealist knows just as well as anyone that ideals are not directly applicable in practice, but he knows too that life must be shaped in conformity with those ideals. People who cannot convince themselves of this truth only show that their help has not been called upon in the shaping of events! One can, therefore, only wish them rain and sunshine in due season and—if possible—good digestion!"

This is intended to show the relationship between idealism and actual practical life, which is called into service, for example, in the building of a bridge. The art of engineering that brings a bridge into being is certainly not controlled by ideas that originate in matter. As the finished bridge must first exist ideally and can only become a real practical bridge after it has been well worked out in thought, so must idealism be something practical, springing from inner practical perception. We must have the instinct, the feeling, that will enable us to carry into actual practical life such objective laws, for instance, as govern the art of engineering. Then it will no longer be asked how these things can be carried out in practical life. For when enough people understand these ideas, they will forthwith put them into practice in actions and deeds. We often hear people say that these ideas are beautiful in many respects, and if realized would be very fine, but humanity is not yet ready for them. The masses, they say, are not yet ripe. Let us see what is really meant by such an assertion. He who knows the relationship of idea to actuality, who understands practical life according to the character of its reality, judges the masses differently. He knows that there are enough people now who, if they only go deeply enough into their own inner natures, can bring full understanding to bear on the matters with which we have dealt. The greatest hindrance is the lack of courage. The energy is lacking to urge them forward to what they might attain if they could only develop in themselves full self-consciousness. Above all, we need to correct something within ourselves; of this practically every human being is capable, if he only gives heed to reality. While people fall into materialism and even take a delight in it, they also fall prey to abstractions, and will not penetrate to reality. Even in external life people are convinced that they are of a practical turn of mind, but they take no trouble to see things so as to recognize their real character.

For instance, suppose that someone comes across a new assertion and believes it. He accepts only its abstract content, and in doing so he may become estranged from life, instead of understanding it better. The writing of a fine editorial presents no great difficulty nowadays because there is so much commonplace in modern civilization that only a small amount of routine is required to enable a person to write phrase after phrase. It is not the point whether or not we agree with the literal meaning of an article nowadays, but it is important that we should be able to judge the extent to which this meaning accords with reality. In this respect there is much to be corrected in the present day. One is impelled to say that what people should demand today above all things is truth, which they should courageously unite with reality. Here are two examples of what is meant.

You may read statistical reports, perhaps of the Balkan States since it has become usual to acquaint oneself with the conditions prevailing in the world, to pass judgments on political situations and similar matters. We can judge of the way in which people gain their information by reading statistics, let us say, of the Balkan States. We read that there are so many Greeks, so many Bulgarians, and then we can calculate how far the claims of the various elements, Greeks, Bulgarians, or Serbians, can be justified. If we then examine the details more closely and compare what we have gained through abstract knowledge about the number of Bulgarians, Serbians, and Greeks in Macedonia, we often find that the father of a family is registered as a Greek, one son as a Bulgarian and another as a Serb. Now one would like to know how this agrees with the truth. Can the family be really so constituted that the father is a Greek, one son a Bulgarian, and another a Serb? * Can we learn anything as to the reality from statistics made in this way? Most of the statistical reports in the world are made after this fashion, especially in commercial life.

Because people do not always feel the necessity of pressing forward through the actual words to the truth of what they hear, they commonly misjudge things. They do not examine closely enough into facts. They are content with the mere surface of life, which is only a covering for the true reality. Today, the first necessity is not to waste time in discussing whether humanity is ripe or unripe, but to point out where the principal evils lie. Once discover and take the trouble to disclose these evils and indicate with sufficient energy the way to deal with them, then people will realize them quickly enough!

Here is a second example. At the beginning of June 1917 the world could read the speech pronounced by the then Emperor Karl of Austria on his accession to the throne. In that speech from the throne there was a great deal said, appropriately at that time, about democracy. Again and again democracy was the theme. Now I have

---

* The truth of this is to be found in the fact that in the Balkan States the blood tie is often not the thing that makes a man a Greek, a Bulgarian, or a Serbian, but his church affiliation. Greek Church, Bulgarian Church, Serbian Church. (Ed.)

read a good deal about this speech, about the enthusiasm with which it was received by the people, and how splendid it was to proclaim democracy to the world at such a time. Taking this speech from beginning to end and looking merely at its literal content, from the journalistic standpoint it was a fine achievement, if we confine ourselves to the style and composition of the sentences, calculated to call forth feelings of pleasure and gratification. Very good! But let us look at the truth! Let us place this speech in its milieu. Then we must ask, "*Who* is speaking thus and in what surroundings?" There we may see, standing in the medieval splendor of his coronation robes, glittering with jewels, the despotic ruler of bygone days, making no attempt to hide his magnificence, surrounded by his brilliant gold-laced paladins. The Middle Ages, complete in all the ceremonial, which, had it spoken truly, would have chosen another subject than democracy!

What is a speech on democracy, however beautiful the words, delivered in the midst of such medieval magnificence? A world-historical lie. From the literal content of the things of the present, we must go back to a perception of the reality. It is not enough to grasp things with the intellect; one must see things as they really are. This is just what spiritual science demands. We cannot deceive ourselves as to the outer reality without paying the penalty. He who would know the spiritual reality in the true sense of spiritual science, as it is taught here, he who would behold the spiritual world, must, above all things, accustom himself to the most absolute truth in the world of the senses. He must yield to no deception regarding all that takes place around him in the world of his five senses. Especially he who would penetrate into the spiritual world must use his five senses in a true and sane manner, and must not give himself up to fantastic thought, as do the many businessmen, the so-called practical people, so much admired, to whom the whole world defers. What we want is not a lamentation over the immaturity of the people, but to show them that we must be true in our inmost soul. Then we should cease to hear continually that untrue talk about the spirit, the spirit. Then will these falsehoods about the difference between right and might be no longer heard throughout the world, but we shall hear of work being done that consists in striving to attain the spirit. Then we shall hear that the spirit so striven after has been won and that men are living a common life together in which they find equal rights for everyone. Only then can we speak of the manner in which an economic system, spiritualized throughout and pervaded with the spirit of equity, will be able to establish the true and real Commonwealth.

It is much more essential that we should recognize the fact that a sufficient number of people are here who at least look within and take themselves in hand, who can have an inner understanding of such hints as I have given. We must never weary of emphasizing these things. We must not, however, think that the mere repetition of phrases to the effect that the spirit must govern the world will bring about, as by enchantment, the coming of the spirit. No! By the work of the human spirit alone can that spirit come into the world. In this respect also we must be true. We must not allow the falsehood to ring through the world that the spirit must come. The truth must be proclaimed that the spirit will not appear until there are places in which not only the materialistic study of outer nature will be carried on, but in which a spiritual conception of life will be striven after.

Out of that spiritual conception of the world must proceed a real social understanding of the habits of life of all humanity in the present and the near future. Everything depends on the fact that people become true with regard to the spirit and to their spiritual endeavor, for the spirit can only be found on the path of truth. It is no excuse, or, rather, it is only an excuse, to say that people are ignorant. In spiritual striving it is important to know that a lie, unconsciously persisted in, causes just as much harm as a lie consciously repeated. It is the duty of man at the present day to elevate his subconsciousness in order to root out falsehood in every realm, even in that of the subconscious. For this reason I should like to conclude with words that are, indeed, truly and earnestly meant. I can well imagine that even after I have attempted to describe the structure of the social organism from the most varied points of view, as it must appear to the eye of the spiritual scientist in its relation to its threefoldness, I can well imagine that there may still be people who will say that these are only ideas. How is it possible, they ask, that people can now rise to such ideas? A gulf yawns between these ideas and those generally understood at the present day. I would only remark that, with regard to such opinions, our answer must be that it need not concern us how advanced or otherwise people are. We need only speak out over and over again what we hold to be the truth, and what we think is likely to bear fruit, and then wait till they have understood. If we do so, if we never tire of repeating this again and again, then people will advance more rapidly than if they are continually told of their immaturity. I believe that the world may soon be ready for such things. I would, therefore, never tire of repeating over and over again what I believe would hasten the advancement of humanity to maturity.

151